Saint Michael's Abbey Press
Saint Michael's Abbey
Farnborough
Hampshire GU14 7NQ

Telephone +44 (0) 1252 546 105
Facsimile +44 (0) 1252 372 822

www.farnboroughabbey.org
prior@farnboroughabbey.org

www.theabbeyshop.com

Original Edition:

Notions sur la Vie Religieuse et Monastique (1885)

New Edition: Saint Michael's Abbey Press, 2006

ISBN 0 907077 48 X

A catalogue record for this book is available from the British Library.

Printed and bound by Newton Printing Ltd., London.

ADTENDITE AD PETRAM UNDE EXCISI ESTIS

This volume is humbly dedicated to the
Abbot and Community of St Pierre de Solesmes.

A number of religious houses have asked us to share with them the instructions Dom Guéranger left us for the training of novices. This we do gladly, convinced as we are that the study of these few pages will be of benefit to the reader.

Dom Charles Couturier
Abbot of Solesmes

Feast of the Ascension, 14th May 1885

Contents

Preface to the New Edition

DOM Guéranger's *Règlement du Noviciat,* written in 1856-57 and published thirty years later under the title *Notions sur la vie religieuse et monastique,* is in a long line of writings destined for Novices, or for those charged with their instruction. These first appeared in the Middle Ages with the *Instructio novitiorum* from eleventh century Canterbury, Adam of Perseigne's *Letters* 5, 17, Stephen of Sawley's *A Mirror for Novices,* Hugh of St Victor's *De Institutione novitiorum,* St Bonaventure's *Regula novitiorum* and Denys the Carthusian's *Exhortatorium novitiorum.*

Dom Guéranger's work was written for his own Novice-Master Dom Charles Couturier, who would succeed him as second abbot of Solesmes. Named Novice-Master less than a month after his profession, Dom Couturier asked his abbot for a document to serve as a basis for his teaching, and a particular rule for the novices themselves: to initiate them into the observances, to shape their behaviour, to guide them in the practice of the spiritual life, and to help in times of trial. In a journal written during this period at Solesmes, Dom Laurence Shepherd, monk of Ampleforth and chaplain at Stanbrook, noted: 'The Abbot is writing a *Règlement du Noviciat* to give him courage.' It was at the request of numerous religious houses that Dom Couturier decided to publish this work in 1885. It was translated into English in 1908 by Dom Jerome Veth of Conception Abbey, USA, into Spanish by a monk of Monserrat, and Italian by the monks of the abbey of St George in Venice.

The Novice as Christian

The first thing that strikes a reader of these pages is Dom Guéranger's insistence on the greatness of the religious state. For him, the religious life, like the Church itself, is a prolongation

of the Incarnation: 'God has done nothing greater than the
Incarnation of which the Church is the prolongation. Now the
Church has a heart: the religious state. That is the most complete
manifestation that there can be here below of the mystery of
the Incarnation, by its exact reproduction of the life of Christ.'[1]
The religious life is presented by Dom Guéranger as a special
way of living out the Incarnation. It desires to imitate as closely
as possible the life Our Lord lived on earth.[2] 'To find grace
Earth has constantly to reflect in the sight of God the image of
His divine Son, given concrete form in humanity' (*chapter* x).

This is not to say that the religious is a different kind
of Christian. The religious life is 'the perfect form of
Christianity' (III). By this he meant that the monastic life keeps
alive in the Church certain values; it points to what every
Christian is. The monk is just an ordinary Christian who lives
the Christian life to the full. 'The monk is simply someone
who takes his Christianity seriously.'[3] The religious life makes
explicit the principal duty of every person dedicated to God.
This programme was outlined and begun at our baptism; the
monastic life touches the mystery of transformation whereby
God turns us into a new being. 'We are baptised only in order

---

[1] Unpublished conference.

[2] See Vita Consecrata: '... that form of life which He, as Son of God, accepted
in entering this world' *(VC 16)*. The evangelical counsels, by which Christ
invites some people to share his experience ... call for and make manifest in
those who accept them 'an explicit desire to be totally conformed to him'
(VC 18). The consecrated life constitutes 'a living memory, a living tradition
of the life and message of the Lord' *(VC 22)*.

[3] Unpublished conference. Compare John Paul II who called monasticism
'a signpost for all the baptised ... a symbolic synthesis of all Christianity ...
when God's call is total as it is in the monastic life, then the person can reach
the highest point that sensitivity, culture and spirituality are able to express'
(Orientale Lumen).

'I am in fact convinced that the monastic experience constitutes the heart
of Christian life, so much so that it can be proposed as a point of reference
for all the baptised ... Monks and nuns are *the Gospel memory* for Christians
in the world' *(25 May 2002)*.

to attain sanctity, and we make profession in order to reach a greater sanctity still.' The religious life is a particular refinement of our baptismal promise, of Christian discipleship and the on-going call to repentance, service and prayer and listening that belong to all Christians. It is ultimately a commitment to a life *per ducatum evangelii*, to a life in the spirit of the beatitudes and the Sermon on the Mount. The religious desires to follow Christ in the spirit of the gospel by faithfully living the monastic life, by renouncing all that might impede one in following him, all that might obscure one's clarity of intent or obscure one's resolve; and by allowing oneself to be transformed into Him.

For Dom Guéranger, to commit ourselves to religious life is to commit ourselves not to be perfect but to pursue perfection. In saying this, Dom Guéranger does not ignore the universal call to holiness on which the Second Vatican Council insists. Every Christian, he says, 'has a real duty of striving to practise perfection, according to the graces he may receive' (VIII).[4] But the religious pledges himself under vow to strive towards this perfection, to grow towards the perfect love of God and neighbour by the practice of the counsels. It is a question of becoming perfectly in fact what we are already: children of God. It is the commitment to becoming a completely new man in the Pauline sense, so that the monk can say 'I live now, not I, but Christ liveth in me.'

The perfection of love is never arrived at with complete success, but what matters is that the monk is always advancing. 'Yet they will comfort themselves with the reflection that the perfection they have attained is not of this world, and that even the greatest saints have only fully realised it in heaven. What has made them saints is their continuing desire for perfection, a desire and tending never weakened by their faults and imperfections' (VIII). The process of becoming a monk or nun

---

[4] 'All the faithful of whatever state or manner of life are called to the fullness of the Christian life and the perfection of charity' *Lumen Gentium*.

lasts as long as life itself; there is no time at which one can say, 'I am now a monk, my formation is finished.' The gift of a vocation is not merely a vocation to the single act of becoming a monk, or entering a noviciate, or making profession. It is a vocation to be a monk who grows; it is a vocation to use the monastic life to grow into the perfect love of God and neighbour. The monk is a novice for his whole life. An authentic monk is always on the road to holiness, always tending towards perfection, towards the heavenly Jerusalem and the encounter with his Creator.

The Novice as Disciple

It is through the practice of the evangelical counsels that the novice's configuration to the Christ is realised: these 'reproduce in us the features of the Incarnate Son of God' (x). The vows are based on the teaching and example of Christ and are a divine gift, like the sacraments which the Church has received from her Lord. As we find in the Gospel, and from the very beginning of the Church's life and history, there have been men and women who wish to dedicate themselves to a closer following of Christ: Jesus Christ was given to us, insists Dom Guéranger, not only as Redeemer, but also as model. 'These divine counsels deserve our respect on account of the way they establish a union between our Lord and the person practising them' (x); 'In Him we can recognise what we ought to be in order to resemble God once more' (IX). Through this constant and loving study of Him, Mary succeeded in realising within herself the pattern of her divine Son and rose to perfection (IX). Mary is not only the model for religious; according to her vocation as Mother she continues to aid, assist and protect the novice, as a result of her perfect communion with her Son.

The evangelical counsels then are the means to the end of perfect discipleship, a state of undivided love in the form of poverty, chastity and obedience. For those whom the Lord calls to this closer following, the counsels are a form of living, the most effective way of letting ourselves go in love, of 'close familiarity with Jesus Christ' and 'co-operation with his mission' (x) surrendering ourselves to the service of God's plan of redemption. They are an expression of the attempt to surrender ourselves, and are also a reminder to persevere in that self-surrender. Moreover , they are also the means by which we are conformed to Christ, the way of 'having the same mind as Christ' (Phil 2:5); they express Christ's personal way of thinking and living. The counsels are not framed in view of man and his possibilities, but in view of Christ and what is possible to God. The follower and imitator of Christ is initiated into the attitude of God. The religious imitates the poor Christ by 'holy poverty is the first degree in the perfect imitation of our Saviour. He was born in a borrowed stable; worked by the sweat of his brow . . . lived on alms while He was preaching; He was nailed naked to the Cross, and his body was laid to rest in a borrowed tomb.' He imitates Christ infinitely pure; chastity 'brings about the establishment of an eternal relationship with God.' By the vow of obedience, Our Lord is perpetuated in those who, like him, renounce their own will to do the will of the Father. 'As it derives from the free decision that the religious has made,' obedience causes the novice 'to renounce his whole self'; it is 'a surrender made into the hands of God,' 'a freely-offered and consecrated holocaust.'

Dom Guéranger also considers the vows from the point of view of 'remedies' which counter three obstacles to man's union with God: poverty challenges 'the attachment, lawful though it may be, to earthly possessions, which chains man to the goods of this world'; chastity, 'the pleasures of the senses, which divide man's heart between God and the creature'; while obedience curbs 'self-will which disturbs the harmony between the will of God and the will of man.' The three counsels constitute all that the creature has to give. The evangelical counsels aim at man's renewal and liberation, a return to man's original state of liberty: 'The attachment to material goods, to creatures and self being successfully fought by the exact observance of the holy vows, the soul finds again its primitive liberty, and tends with ease towards its divine centre' (VII). They therefore signify a total belonging to God, a way of giving up everything to follow Christ: exterior goods, goods of the body, and even one's own freedom and will. While affirming the value of created goods, the monastic life shows their relative character by pointing to God as the absolute good. The vows offer a 'remedy' for humanity because they reject the idolatry of anything created and make visible the living God. Through the practice of the vows the religious purifies himself and comes to union with God through the imitation of Jesus Christ.

The religious life is a total gift of self given not once but accomplished over a lifetime. 'This imitation of the man-God, this incorporation with Jesus Christ is undoubtedly a hard task, and costs nature many a sacrifice' (x). Those who seek to follow Christ open themselves to the onslaught of demons, deceitful agents opposed to the true God and to his Christ and to all those who seek to live good lives. The early monks and nuns considered the spiritual life as an invisible war, triumphantly begun by Christ in the desert. They felt themselves called to fight with him and like him. This imagery appears both in the Rule of St Benedict and in Dom Guéranger. The victory of Christ's cross is something each must make his own. And the cross shows that sin and wickedness are not invincible; evil can be overcome. In all this, the message is: do not fear. Dom Guéranger insists that far from fearing, the monk is to have a joyous, unlimited confidence in the power of Christ, to count on his aid, to hope for an eternal reward. Thanks to the power of Christ, the novice grows through his struggles and advances further along the way of purity of heart. Throughout this work, Dom Guéranger enters into the novices' trials, temptations and weaknesses, offers practical suggestions for breaking bad habits, and encourages them to defuse situations by recognising the grace of God ever at their disposal and accepting that they cannot reform themselves by sheer will-power.

The Novice as Lover

For Dom Guéranger, the Christian life and the religious life imply a living faith, operating through hope and love to unite the soul to God. By faith, he means not only belief, what is held as true, but also personal commitment, a holding fast to what is true, throughout the ups and downs of life. It is the habit of seeing our life in relation to God, referring everything to Him; through faith 'the eyes of those faithful to grace are opened by this divine light, and all things appear in a pure and fuller aspect.' For Dom Guéranger, the novice is to be above all a person of faith: 'Faith must be his element, his nourishment, his joy, his delight; for it is first and principally by faith that God communicates Himself to man and transforms and supernaturalizes his life.' Faith is not only the way in which the monk cleaves to God; it also enables God's power and omnipotence to be realised so that he can do great things in the novice's life. The person who believes participates in God's power.

If faith opens the eyes to the divine light, so that 'the world and this present life are transformed,' hope is 'the firm and unshakeable trust' in the unchanging reality of God. Ever practical, Dom Guéranger puts the novice on guard against two dangers to hope: lack of confidence and presumption, and vividly portrays the temptations to discouragement or complacency that 'the old serpent' seeks to arouse in his heart.

Religious fulfil to the highest degree the love of God and of our Lord Jesus Christ, making it the full meaning of their life and loving in God all their brothers and sisters. They move towards the perfection of charity, choosing God as their one thing necessary. By charity, we love as God loves, consciously enter into the disposition and attitude of God of love whose self-giving is of His very essence. Thus faith, hope and love are forms of sharing in the divine life, each penetrating and enhancing the other, to form in us a state of loving, active surrender to God. This is the way of Jesus, and the new life he gives at baptism and religious life means that it must become our way of spending ourselves, offering ourselves to God and others in a love like His. In his Son, as Dom Guéranger loves to repeat, God bestows things on us without measure. But He does this to the end that we will learn to give ourselves without calculating.

The Novice as Monk

Religious life is a life dedicated while renouncing even good things – property, family, personal independence – so as to cleave to Christ more wholeheartedly and be free for his service. Because the monastic life has no secondary ends, such as teaching or nursing, it points to the essence of all religious life. That is why Dom Guéranger sees in the monastic life 'the most excellent and complete form' of the religious life (III). The monastic life is the original form of consecrated life, the first to establish itself with rules and vows, and for some ten centuries it was the only form of religious life in the Church. And it is the one form of religious life common to East and West 'Monasticism is a form of Christianity as old as the Church herself. It was born in the East with our faith.'[5] In the monastic life we encounter an uninterrupted tradition that goes back to the earliest centuries of the Church.

By their true vocation, monks are called to solitude, 'to separation from the world, by their enclosure and by their habit' (I), as Dom Guéranger writes, to fulfill the Lord's saying about leaving all to follow Him. The cloister favours the solitude of the monk with God. There he seeks the company of God,

---

[5] Dom Guéranger, unpublished life of Saint Benedict.

and intimacy with the Three divine Persons, and thanks to this intimacy, a real union with all other men and women.

The novice who follows the Rule of St Benedict unites to his solitude the practice of fraternal charity at the heart of a community. The monk, he insists, 'cannot arrive at the perfection proper to his state without including zeal for his neighbour. . . Monastic life tends to draw man nearer to God by submission and love.' By neighbour Dom Guéranger means not only the members of one's own community but also the Church and the world. The monk is 'a universal intercessor,' and must be filled with 'apostolic zeal' for the salvation of souls. He leads a communal life; he needs others to eliminate his egoism; he benefits from their counsel, their example, their teaching, their direction, their support; he learns to love God through the Rule and the common life. 'Take pleasure in the company of your brethren, because the Holy Spirit has chosen and united you for one and the same end; let the joys as well as the sorrows be held in common.' The community enables him to practise and to prove the reality of his love for his neighbour. Each Benedictine monastery forms a family under the paternal guidance of the Abbot. The true character of life at Solesmes under Dom Guéranger was familial, and he himself was above all a father, firm and gentle, setting before his monks, nuns and guests the highest spiritual ideals, while showing a tender and even humorous patience with human weakness.

Monks have no other end than to seek God, by a life of contemplation and renunciation. For Dom Guéranger, the divine office is both the pre-eminent means to and expression of that end. 'The brethren will esteem nothing more than the divine service,' writes Dom Guéranger, 'and they will regard it as the most noble and useful employment of the day. They will understand that having left all for God, their first care must be concerned with God.' The Divine Office remains the heart of a monastic community's life, the perfect expression of a life given over wholly to the service of God. The Divine Office is the setting and the occasion when the novice reaffirms, both inwardly and outwardly that choice of God which each one made when entering the monastery, the choice to serve God first and foremost in the school of his service

The Divine Office then is the centre of the monk's life; all else flows from it and leads back to it. After the Mass and the Sacraments, it is 'the most profitable and holy work performed on earth.' Dom Guéranger calls the prayers of the liturgy 'hidden manna which strengthens the soul and endows it with understanding for the holy things of God.' The liturgy is the novice's great school of prayer, embracing the prayer life of the Church and of each individual. It can help to create in the novice the mind of the Church, expanding his personal prayer, making it more generous and universal. The office is the community's prayer, in which the whole Church is represented. Dom Guéranger reminds the novice that Church uses the chant at the Divine Office to express the love of the Church toward her Bridegroom, Christ.[6]

But Dom Guéranger also alerts the novice to the ascesis of choir; the need for self-control, humility, attention; the struggle against distractions, discouragement, and doubts about the value of it all. Dom Guéranger exhorts the novice to 'endure with joy its blessed hardships.' It is good that the central act of our day should make such demands: the Office is a sacrifice of praise; it is also a sacrifice of self.

For Dom Guéranger, the Rule of St Benedict is not only indispensable, it is central; it is the reality which has constantly

---

[6] Communities of monks and nuns, says the Second Vatican Council, 'represent in a special way the Church at prayer. They are a fuller sign of the Church as it continually praises God with one voice, and they fulfil the duty of working to build up and increase the whole mystical Body of Christ and for the good of the local churches above all by their prayer' (*Sacrosanctum Concilium*, 99). The prayer of monks and nuns is recognized by the Church as offered in her name; it is therefore the Church's prayer; 'by offering these praises to God they are standing before God's throne in the name of the Church, their Mother' (SC 85).

to be adverted to, the universal point of reference: 'It is by the Rule of St Benedict that we will be Benedictines' (II). While recognizing the need for modifications in changed circumstances, Dom Guéranger recognises that a true fidelity to the spirit of the Rule is going to involve a certain literalism; the spirit of the monastic life is inseparable from the concrete observances in which it is realized. The Rule is the clearest expression of the terms of the life to which the novices engage themselves; it must be repeatedly presented to them 'so that they may know on what they are entering' *(Rule, chapter 58)*. The one who enters monastic life studies the Rule and sees how it is lived in the monastery to see if he can identify with it, if his way is to be found therein. To become a monk is equivalent to embracing the whole way of life as set out by the Rule.

The Christian as Novice

Lay people today, both in the Church and outside it, are eager for spiritual guidance, long to develop a life of prayer, and be guided in the way of holiness. There is much practical advice to be gained here in Dom Guéranger's teaching on the imitation of Christ, on faith, hope and love, the life of prayer and the liturgy, fraternal charity, and the struggles of the spiritual life. Dom Guéranger also insists in this work that the way of the counsels belongs as much to lay people as religious: 'Even in the midst of the world, the practice of Christian life would be impossible without rising, in certain instances, to the observance of the counsels' (X). As an expression of Christ's own life, poverty, chastity and obedience are not something one can take or leave. The practice of the counsels, at least in spirit, belongs to the Christian life as such. All must respond to the words and teaching of Jesus, each in his own way. Both the monk and the Christian in the world are called to be an *alter Christus* (another Christ).

A Christian's whole life is a noviciate for eternity. In offering this new translation, the first since 1908, the monks of Farnborough are not merely making available an historical document, but offering what they hope will be something useful for our daily life. Perhaps the last word should be Dom Guéranger's:

'Pray without ceasing that Jesus Christ be accomplished in you; that His life find its expression in your lives and animate your whole being' (IX).

By a Benedictine of St Cecilia's Abbey, Ryde

30 January 2006

Anniversary of the death of Dom Guéranger

The Essence of the Religious Life

The religious life has three principal aims:

Repentance for sins that have been committed: that is why it is called 'conversion.'

Imitation of Jesus Christ by putting into practice His teachings and counsels, so that the religious becomes like Him.

Union with God even in this world, through charity. Now, this union can only take place to the extent that certain obstacles within man are removed. These obstacles are of three kinds:

The attachment, even legitimate, to *worldly possessions*, which binds a man to the things of this world.

The attachment, even legitimate, to *sensual pleasures*, which leaves man divided between God and creatures.

The attachment, even legitimate, to our *own will*, which disturbs the harmony between the will of God and the will of man.

Real renunciation by *spiritual and material poverty* removes the obstacle presented by attachment to earthly things.

Sincere *obedience* to another's will, with the will of God in mind, removes the obstacle presented by self-will.

Complete *chastity* of body, mind and heart removes the obstacle presented by sensual pleasures.

Since the religious life is not a transitory action, but a state of life, then *poverty*, *chastity* and *obedience* should become second nature for those who profess it, and inseparable from them; this is what happens when someone takes perpetual vows, which are essential for a man to be established in the religious state.

When he has entered the permanent religious state, man is in a position to strive towards perfection. Now, perfection consists in the love of God, or charity; and charity brings about the union of the soul with God.

Religious life also results in the *imitation of Jesus Christ*, for the Saviour's whole life offers us an expression of the three virtues which are the subject of the vows.

Finally, the religious life brings about a complete *conversion of life and behaviour*, and *true repentance* in those who profess it; for to deal with the three sicknesses of sinful man it offers three effective remedies, and when these are applied they both atone for sin and lead to the acquiring of the virtues which combat sin.

That is the overall idea which brothers ought to have of religion, and on which they ought continually to meditate, as this is the goal they are setting themselves when they enter the Novitiate.

Now, since they are going to have to practise the religious state within the monastic life, it is important for them to get to know that life, which is the form in which they will dedicate themselves to God in the religious state.

chapter I

The Essence of the Monastic Life

The main features of the monastic life are these:

i.   separation from the world through withdrawal and the monastic habit;
ii. the daily solemn celebration of the Divine Office;
iii. work;
iv. the mortifying of the body;
v.   life as a family;
vi. works of religious zeal for the benefit of one's neighbour, if obedience allows or prescribes them.

Having put forward this definition of the monastic life, we must now proceed to explain in detail to the brothers its various elements, and the way in which it is put into practice in the Novitiate.

§ I

on separation from the world

THE monastic life is, by its very nature, a life apart and requires that those who profess it should live within the monastic enclosure. Their separation from the world must be real to fulfil the saying of Jesus Christ, 'Anyone who has left his father or mother . . .' or, again, 'Come, follow me.' That is why the monastic spirit is a spirit of retreat, and the expression of this is monastic enclosure.

The brothers ought therefore to think of the monastery as the place where they will remain until they die, and they should love this withdrawn way of life, so that if, after profession, obedience authorises them to return to the world from time to time, their love for their enclosure will be in no way diminished.

They should look on the separation from their family, with which they will henceforth have to live, as an essential fulfilment of the counsels of Jesus Christ. This separation ought to be the touchstone for their vocation as well as that sacrifice on which their religious life rests, as on a foundation-stone.

Yet in consenting to live apart from their relations, they should avoid any idea that a perfect religious ought to repudiate all affection for them. On the contrary, purified by divine charity, this affection, will only become more lively, tender, and faithful. What is said here about family will equally apply to any friends they have left in the world, provided that the relationship with them is straightforward and virtuous.

Although they live within the novitiate, occasions may arise when they will have something to do with the outside world. In this respect, each order has its own rules, which the novices need to know and take care to keep.

Yet since the outward form of enclosure is of little use unless the spirit of the world is banished from our hearts, the brothers should try to subdue any worldly memories they may have; their way of seeing everything will be in accordance with the spirit of the religious life, which is opposed to the spirit of the world; they should avoid giving any impression of worldliness, and without affectation they should show in the way they talk and act, the gravity, modesty and good manners which are suited to the state of life they wish to embrace. In their relations with people outside they should take care to distance themselves from any worldly spirit, and in all things they should behave in such a way as only to edify people.

As the religious habit is the visible sign of their separation from the world, the brothers will regard it with the highest respect and will wear it in this spirit; they will try to keep it as clean as possible, and only take it off when really necessary, and will never appear outside their cells without it.

§ II

on the divine office

THE brothers should consider nothing more important than the *Divine Office*, and will look upon it as the noblest and most useful thing they do in the course of the day. They will understand that, having left everything behind for the sake of God, their first concern ought to be waiting upon God.

The zeal they display for divine service will show how far they are faithful to their vocation. This zeal will manifest itself not only in their faithful presence in choir, but also in the care they take to learn the rules for the divine office, for the chant and for the ceremonies.

They should not be contented merely with conscientiously following the instruction of the rubrics and text of the Breviary; but should also pay devoted attention to the way the office is carried out, so as to learn how to do it later. They will take note of the pitch, the inflections of voice, and the manner of proceding in all the ceremonies, both general and particular. They will avoid thinking of this preoccupation as a distraction, but will frequently ask God that they may carry out His service with dignity, reverence, modesty and exactness.

They should zealously devote themselves to studying plainchant, with the sole aim of glorifying God, and will generously resist any natural dislike they might feel for it, recalling that God will take this into account. And even if they do not arrive at great perfection in this respect, it will be a considerable achievement to have diminished the difficulties which might be occasioned by their voices.

With regard to the readings in choir, they should try to observe the exact quantities and accentuation of the syllables, and not let themselves become discouraged, however much they may previously have neglected this essential matter.

When they are carrying out some duty, they should always be sure to prepare for this, so that if they should happen to do something wrong, they will not have to answer for it before God's majesty. In short, they will show such a religious keenness to learn everything, that we may expect to be edified by their conduct after profession, when called on to carry out the duty of hebdomadary.[7]

The brothers must take care to recollect themselves before the Divine Office, using the few moments they spend at the *statio*[8] to lift up their hearts to God, preparing to appear before Him; and when they enter the church, they should avoid anything that might distract them. When they have taken their places, they should make the necessary preparations, and banish any thoughts unconnected with the praise of God. They should try to pay attention to the chant and sacred ceremonies so as to be edified by them, avoiding at the same time all movements or looks that would only distract them from the great object which should occupy their thoughts.

They should make the various bows – whether a small, medium or profound bow – with an inner devotion and not merely in a perfunctory way; at the end of the Psalms and hymns they should have the deliberate intention of honouring the Holy Trinity, which is always associated with the mystery being celebrated, or the saint honoured on that particular day.

They should love the Psalms which constituted, as it were, the daily bread of the saints of our order, convinced that if they become familiar with them, they will have taken a great step

---

[7.] The monk appointed to presiding at the divine office for a given week.
[8.] The gathering of the monks in silent preparation for the procession into the church for the office.

along the way towards contemplative prayer. They ought to request this grace from God, and likewise that of understanding and enjoying the other parts of the divine office.

When singing or reciting the words, they should try to understand their meaning so as to make it their own. They should gently try to discern the allusions made by Holy Church in the wording of the Liturgy, that they may feed upon this hidden manna, which strengthens the soul and grants it understanding of the things of God. They should love to re-live, in the course of the day, the impressions the Holy Spirit may have granted them on such occasions, so that they may deserve to receive new ones.

They will follow with reverent attention the various pieces that the hebdomadary sings or recites, and above all the collect for the day, which they will take particularly to heart. They will make sure not to omit any of the bows which are made during the prayers, the Epistles, the Gospels, and other readings.

The brothers will bear in mind that the Church makes constant use of chant in divine service to express the ardour of the feelings which the Holy Spirit arouses in her. They will draw the conclusion that the disposition with which they approach the celebration of the Divine Office should be one of enthusiasm for the divine mysteries, and they will try to realize within themselves the saying of our blessed Father, St Benedict, when he asks that 'Mind and voice be in harmony.'

They should sing with interest, docility and humility, without being in any way lifeless, vain, or stubborn in sticking to their own ideas, recalling that chant carelessly performed, or tarnished by human pretentiousness, is not pleasing to God. They should remember that their song is destined to mingle with that of the angels, and this thought will induce them to keep natural inclinations in check while they are performing such a sacred task.

The brothers's opinion of the divine service to which they are dedicated will then be all the higher, as this supreme homage due to God's majesty has become less common in our own day on account of the violent and sacrilegious suppression of so many monasteries and cathedral chapters, where previously everywhere the praise of God had been sung. They will often give thanks to the Lord, that He has deigned to choose them to inherit and hand on to others the traditions of public worship; and will join with the prophet in asking Him to graciously multiply, and not diminish, the voices of those who celebrate His holy name.

With holy zeal, they should banish that worldly notion that the time they spend in choir would be more usefully employed in study or in other religious activities, as if there could be any work comparable to liturgical prayer in dignity, importance or efficacy: as if the prayer of the Church, offered up to God under conditions which she herself has laid down, were not (after the Holy Sacrifice, and the administration of the Sacraments) the most useful and most sacred work carried out on earth.

Far from allowing themselves to entertain such unworthy thoughts, naturalist in character and thus dangerous, the brothers should rather deplore thier inability to imitate the holy fervour of our fathers, who rose in the night to sing the Divine Office, and who devoted much more time to it in the daytime than we manage to do.

This thought will motivate them to be zealous in performing what the Constitutions prescribe for the Divine Office, and they will gladly suffer that sacred fatigue which is sometimes involved in celebrating the great ceremonies.

§ III

on monastic work

MONASTIC life is carried on two wings: these two wings are the *Divine Office* and *work*. In the Divine Office we wait on God; through working we fruitfully occupy those hours which the weakness of our spirit prevents us from devoting to contemplation.

Monastic work is, therefore, a homage rendered to God. That is why it should begin with prayer, and be carried out in a prayerful spirit.

The brothers should learn to love this basic principle of their state of life, and should understand that the monk ought always to have some serious occupation, except in those hours given to recreation; and even these serve only to refresh him, the better to pray and to work.

The brothers should make it a lifelong habit to avoid idleness, which is the enemy of the soul, as our holy Patriarch says. Above all, they will avoid indulging in reveries, which exhaust the soul's strength and gradually stifle our sensitivity for what is divine. They will grasp that being assiduous in their work tames the passions and prevents a whole host of sins; in dedicating each instant of their life to God, they ensure their perseverance and acquire an immense amount of merit. If they do find some difficulty in submitting themselves to work, they will recall that this is a punishment imposed by God Himself on sinful man, and accept this with a humble and courageous heart, just as our ancestors did, when they received this sentence from their Creator. They will bear in mind that the Son of God, when He assumed our human nature, set us an example of working, to teach us that this is one of man's first duties and a powerful means of making reparation.

The brothers will also keep in mind that in order to be meritorious and truly religious, work has to be carried out in accordance with obedience. Natural attraction and human whim may result in work that men praise and appreciate; but the eternal reward will not take those works into account. The brothers will therefore take pleasure in being perfectly obedient where work is concerned, and will be keen to follow exactly the directions given them for the use of their time; and they will do nothing whatever beyond what is directed, without having obtained permission for it.

If they find that they like the work that has been assigned to them, they will try to sanctify that attraction, by frequently offering up to God what they are doing, that He may graciously act within them and through them. If the work assigned to them has little attraction for them, they will recall that they have entered the religious state in order to break with their own will, and that it is always better and safer to go counter to their inclinations than to follow them.

Remembering that they are working for God, who will repay them with interest, they will take care not to carry out this duty as if just trying to get it done, but their diligence will show that they are seeking God in this second means of religious life. In doing so, they will deserve God's help and often find that their assiduous efforts will be blessed from on high and rewarded with unexpected progress.

Monastic work is of two types: *intellectual work* and *manual work*. The first is more excellent when it is directed towards a supernatural end, and is governed by obedience. The second is also of great value because it humbles man's pride and consecrates his body to God's service.

The brothers should practise both, but especially intellectual work. They will set before themselves, as their ultimate aim in their studies and their reading, progress in their knowledge of God and His mysteries, the love of holy Church, and the acquisition of those virtues which make up a true religious. With those dispositions, intellectual work will be of great profit for their spiritual good.

They will, besides, undertake manual work, and will be employed, without distinction, in the humblest services in the house, like sweeping, helping in the kitchen, shoe-cleaning, working in the garden, and so on. The Novice-Master will decide how much time the brothers are to spend on this work, and whether they work together or alone.

§ IV
on the mortification of the body

THE mortification of the body is another essential part of monastic life, and one of its main features. The brothers will therefore esteem this highly, and will be convinced that any rule lacking this element, however pious it might be, could not be placed among the monastic rules.

They will recall the mortifications in the way of life of John the Baptist, the austere practices of the Desert Fathers, the life of our holy Patriarch, and those of all the saints of our Order; and they will become increasingly convinced that the struggle with the flesh, by means of bodily mortification, is a basic principle in the life of any monk.

They will be strengthened in this path by considering the sinner's need to make expiation, when he has entered the religious state so as to effect a conversion in his life and behaviour; the great help to the soul when the flesh is humbled; the illusion of those people who, contrary to the example of the saints, claim to be able to achieve spiritual mortification without mortifying the body; and lastly, the precious benefits of sharing in the sufferings which Jesus Christ endured in his body as well as in his soul.

With this in mind, they will have a sincere love for all the penitential practices that our holy Patriarch established in his holy Rule, especially as relating to abstinence from meat and fasting; and if these venerable and salutary directions have been eased by the Church condescending to our weakness, the brothers will only be the more energetic in their love for what remains to us of these holy practices.

They will show their respect for these precious remnants of the ancient observance in every way and practise them bravely and without delay. They will always speak of them with respect and support them by their example and their faithfulness. If at first their health demands that some allowances be made, they will accept this simply; but they will ask God to come to their help, so that they may soon be able share in the sacred toil of their brothers.

As concerns all those bodily mortifications which are not prescribed by the Constitutions, they will undertake nothing on their own initiative without the explicit permission of the Novice-Master.

The thought of mortification should inspire the brothers to suffer without complaint, even joyfully and happily, those discomforts arising from bad weather, from coarse or badly-prepared food, uncomfortable quarters, illnesses and other minor complaints, or from the practice of the Rule. Nonetheless, if they did have reason to think that their health should be considered, they should confide this to the Novice-Master; having done so, they should leave everything in the hands of God, accepting with complete detachment any alleviation offered to them, or continuing to bear the yoke of the religious life with goodwill, if it was not considered appropriate to make allowance for their weakness.

§ V

on life as a family

MONASTIC life is lived in common, and the Spirit of God has arranged it thus in order that monks may find a powerful help in the example of their brothers and an excellent opportunity for merit in exercising fraternal charity.

The brothers will thus have a very high regard for this family life that they are called to lead, and will try to appreciate its advantages and to foster the spirit of family life within themselves and in each other. They will rejoice to see others sharing in the graces granted to them and develop an affection for one another, as brothers brought together by the same vocation. They will rejoice in each other's company, bearing in mind that it is the Holy Spirit himself who has chosen them and brought them together for a common purpose; they will share their joys as well as their sorrows, and will live together in a familiarity which will in no way diminish the mutual respect they owe one another.

They will encourage each other to persevere and to make progress, and they will offer fervent prayer for any of their number whom they can see is being tempted or tested. They will be careful to avoid any word or gesture which might be damaging for their brothers by leading them to slacken their efforts towards that perfection to which they all aspire.

Besides the inward affection they bear towards one another, the brothers will give visible signs of the mutual charity which unites them and will seek to please one another in all things, each letting the other's wish take precedence, both in words and in practice, and avoiding anything that might suggest personal pretensions. The more senior brothers will take it as their duty to show a humble warmth to the new brothers, and the latter will respond to this with sincere gratitude.

Those of the brothers who might be honoured with the priesthood or one of the higher orders will never make much of this in relation to those who have not received any such honours; they will be sincerely convinced of their own unworthiness of such a high dignity and office.

Since God often allows a vocation to bring together in monasteries people of quite opposite natural dispositions, the brothers will be on their guard against any antipathy which the devil might engender through these differences. They will make every effort to overcome those feelings of distance that he will try to inspire in them in respect of this brother or that; and at the same time they will be on their guard lest they give way to any blind feeling of mere natural sympathy, by which they might feel drawn to one brother or another. They will pay most careful attention, and will correct anything which might injure the family spirit which ought to unite them all.

If any brother becomes aware within himself of a tendency to isolation, a tendency to misanthropy which might make common life uncomfortable for him, then instead of giving rein to this dangerous temptation, he should set himself to overcome it, first of all by prayer, and also by his own courageous and persistent efforts, lest this inclination might bolster his pride, and expose him to the risk of losing his vocation.

The family spirit will lead the brothers to conceive a sincere affection for the Novice-Master, who is the immediate bond of unity and has been appointed by the Superior to be their guide. They will manifest their devout respect for all the monks and see in them so many fathers, in relation to whom they are as yet but children. Lastly, they will have a filial devotion to the Abbot, who represents Jesus Christ within the monastery.

The brothers will also be firmly attached to their Order and constantly ask the Lord in prayer to protect, support, and increase it for His glory and for the salvation and sanctification of souls. They will think highly of the way of life led in the Order. It has been recognised and approved by the Holy See as being in accordance with the spirit of St Benedict, and should therefore be respected by all children of the Church, all the more so by those who have been led by divine grace to enter the Novitiate.

They will never venture the least criticism of the observances, under the pretext that these are more perfect elsewhere; they will remember that they have not yet committed themselves in any way, and so are perfectly free to go wherever their fancy leads them. If it happened that some did not esteem the Order, or its spirit or its administration, they should understand straight away that they will find it impossible to develop this family spirit. It would then be their duty to withdraw, so as not to retain the externals of a life that will never gain the allegiance of their thought and intentions.

This family spirit, which is based on a high regard for the paths Providence has chosen in dealing with themselves, will in no way diminish the pious esteem they owe to all the other rules and constitutions which have been approved by the Holy See. Far from it: they will earnestly pray for the preservation and growth of all the religious orders and take a lively interest in everything that happens to them, for good or for ill.

§ VI

works of religious zeal for the benefit of one's neighbour

ALTHOUGH one of the foundations of the monastic life is separation from the world, the brothers ought to avoid thinking that the monk could achieve perfection in his state of life, if zeal for his neighbour's welfare was lacking in his intentions and behaviour. 'The Lord' says Sirach, 'has made a commandment for every man regarding his neighbour.' The more the monastic life aims at bringing man closer to God through devotion and love, the more the monk, entering into the spirit of his vocation, should be zealous for the salvation of his neighbour; for this is the great, eternal preoccupation of God, since to this end he has given everything, even his own Son.

The brothers should understand that they ought not to enter monastic life to be exclusively concerned with perfecting themselves, regardless of their neighbour's sanctification. Instead, they will reflect that, since the works of holiness carried out in the Church affect, through the communion of saints, the whole of the mystical body of Jesus Christ, every believer's intentions should, by that very fact, extend well beyond their own person. From its very institution by our Lord, the religious life was particularly intended to be, as regards its merits, a treasury of good for all, and the Divine Office, which is the monk's main work, bestows on him the function of universal intercessor. In a word, nothing would be more plainly contrary to charity, which is the hallmark of the followers of Jesus Christ, than a petty preoccupation with one's self which would close a monk's eyes to the needs of those who will always remain his brothers.

They will therefore constantly desire the coming of God's Kingdom, the subject of the second petition in the Lord's Prayer, which includes the conversion of infidels and Jews, the return to the fold of heretics and schismatics, the amendment of sinners, the perseverance of the righteous, and the perfection of those souls whom God has called to a closer union with him while still in this world. With this in view, they will recall that they have been helped and supported by other people in their conversion, and are still being helped to persevere, so they ought not to shut themselves away in the narrowness of their hearts, nor see things differently from the way that God sees and wills. Their desires, intentions, prayers, works of piety and penitence will therefore be offered to God in a spirit of zeal and love for their neighbour's welfare, and this attitude, faithfully maintained in them, will keep them from that spirit of isolation and indifference with which the world has so often reproached those who live in monasteries.

But they will not stop at this hidden and interior attitude. So far as they are able, they will practice apostolic zeal within the Novitiate first of all, in trying by their example, by what they do and say, to maintain and further develop the spirit of religion, and to support anyone who might be wavering in his vocation. As regards their relations and friends in the world, they will – according to the measure of contact that is permitted

– have very much at heart the need to support them in all that is good and remove them from evil or error, if by any misfortune they should take those paths.

Bearing in mind the future way of life which awaits them after they have been consecrated to God by holy profession, they will also prepare themselves for whatever works of zeal may be given them in obedience – whether tasks assigned to them within the monastery; or work in the cause of clarifying the truth in writings aimed at the general public; or the exercise of the sacred ministry, by preaching the word of God and administering the sacraments. Their desire will be that our Lord may be glorified by these various means, and that souls may be saved and sanctified. Even if only a small share of these various works is allotted to them, or if obedience does not require this, they will still resolve to work for the saving of souls by leading an edifying life, which is always a great benefit to Christian society; for the sight of a monastery whose religious serve God with enthusiasm is in itself an eloquent sermon and a powerful means of nourishing and strengthening the principle of supernatural life in every country.

For the same reasons, they will be whole-hearted in commending to God's care those works of zeal carried out within the order, asking God often in prayer to accept and bless them, whether they are directed towards our own concerns within the Order, or those of the general public, or which serve directly the great goal of the salvation of souls. They will frequently ask God that the Order may be filled with men powerful in words and deeds, to His divine glory and for His service, after the example of so many illustrious saints of the monastic order, who became all things to all men, and served both the Church and those souls redeemed in Jesus Christ. The whole lives of these great religious were, at the same time, the most vivid expression of that spirit which our great Patriarch set down in his holy Rule.

Finally, zeal for the welfare of one's neighbour will inspire the brothers with tender compassion for those souls who are in Purgatory. They will recall that it is to the Abbey of Cluny that the suffering Church owes that relief afforded it each year by the Church militant on November 2nd; they will have much at heart the aim of continuing this holy tradition, and will try in every possible way to give help to these souls, who are so dear to God; for although they no longer belong to this world, they nonetheless intently long for that effective help which the mercy of God allows us to offer.

chapter II

On the Excellence of the Rule and its Observance

HAVING explained the essence of the monastic life, we must now expound the excellence of the rule to the brothers and to inspire them with that respect which it deserves. They will easily gain this respect when they reflect that the man who is consecrated to God needs to be strengthened against his own weakness to accomplish what he has promised to God, whether in view of the religious state in general, or the monastic life in particular . They will also grasp that since monks live a common life and form a society, quite precise rules, held in common, are indispensable for the preservation of order and the attainment of the object of the cenobitic life.

Thus it is, that at an early stage in the Church's life, we see the appearance of rules of religious life to satisfy this double need; and their usefulness was so widely recognised that the Church never gives its approval of any religious association, without first having studied and confirmed its rule of life. Hence, holy profession is nowadays always made, not only of the three vows essential to the religious life, but also in accordance with this or that rule that the Church has approved. From this it follows that the life of a religious can only be fully acceptable to God, if it conforms in all respects with the rule according to which he took his vows. Any religious whose life is constantly in conflict with his rule can hardly flatter himself that he is on the way to salvation.

The brothers, then, will have a high opinion of the Rule, and even in the Novitiate onward will be keen to keep it with zeal and understanding. It makes any religious pleasing to God by supporting him in his weakness, and by leading him to bring forth a great number of supernatural works which, without the rule, he might not have achieved. Finally, it secures good order in the community, without which it could not long exist in an edifying way.

By the rule, we should understand not only that holy Rule which our Blessed Father St Benedict bequeathed to us, but also the Constitutions confirmed by the Holy See which adapt the holy Rule to our weakness without altering its spirit, and lastly those rulings and regulations issued by legitimate authority in accordance with the holy Rule and the Constitutions.

The brothers will look upon the holy Rule as the testament of our holy Patriarch and the most precious legacy we have from him. They will treat the volume containing the Rule with respect; they will listen devoutly to its words, in chapter or in the refectory. They will take pleasure in trying to commit it to memory, so far as this is required of them; they will listen in a religious spirit to the explanations and commentaries offered them, whether in the Novitiate or in spiritual conferences; and indeed they will copy out the entire text, in their own hand, during their Postulancy.

They should be convinced that one of the principal sources of grace lies in understanding this admirable book, which has made so many saints and is stamped with the Spirit of God; only God could have inspired our great Patriarch with the charity, discretion, gentleness and power which we admire on every page. The brothers should therefore understand that, if nowadays we fall short of the literal observance of what this holy Rule prescribes, we should at least lack nothing of its spirit; and when our authorised practice is less strict, we should enter all the more into out Holy Patriarch's intentions by accomplishing the little we do in such a way that he may still recognise us as his children. It is by the Rule of St Benedict that we shall be Benedictines: we ought therefore to make an effort to identify ourselves with it in every way and to make it part of our entire life.

Since the main object of the Constitutions is to adapt the holy Rule to the moral and physical weakness of men of our times, the brothers will accord them a sovereign respect, and will try to get to know them well and to observe them exactly.

However, we need to state precisely the extent of the obligations we are called on to undertake. Our brothers should know that, with the exception of those articles of the holy Rule and of the Constitutions which touch on the question of the vows, or are at the same time laid down in canon law, the various regulations to be found in that same holy Rule and Constitutions, do not of themselves demand our obedience upon pain of theological sin. That is the accepted and agreed teaching and is consistent with the doctrine of St Thomas Aquinas, so as not to impose too heavy and too rigorous a yoke upon consciences. At the same time, the brothers must understand that, if these points in the holy Rule and in the Constitutions were flouted in a scornful spirit or in such a manner as gave rise to scandal, then such an offence would become a mortal or a venial sin, according to the degree of the contempt or the scandal.

Although the brothers in the Novitiate are not yet bound by the obligations of the Rule or the vows, they will nonetheless make an effort to practise all the various points of the observance, as if already bound by their Profession. If their physical or moral health required it, a greater indulgence may be accorded them in the course of the Postulancy, so that they may have time to break themselves in, thus avoiding too sudden a transition from one way of life to another. Once they have entered the Novitiate, however, they will all have to conform to the letter of the common and particular observances of the Professed brothers, happy to offer God this pledge of their faithfulness to their vocation.

They will also recall that a Novice who showed himself negligent or unfaithful in his practice of the Rule would thereby run the risk of not being accepted for holy Profession; and if this were to happen, the Novice would bear the most serious responsibility of having lost the means of following the vocation inspired by God, which is one of the greatest dangers which may threaten salvation in this world.

The thought that the bad example set by offences against the Rule might injure their brothers by leading them to do the same will also keep them within the bounds of their duty, and they will all work together for their common edification, by preparing themselves for a holy Profession by perfect fidelity in all things.

chapter III

On the Essential Foundations of Religious Life

HAVING given our brothers the essential ideas concerning the monastic life, we must now turn again to the religious life, which finds in the monastic life its principal and most complete form. The religious state of life, as we have seen, consists of the practice of the three virtues of poverty, chastity, and obedience, by means of which the soul frees itself from all those obstacles which prevent its progress towards perfection, purifies itself from its stains through expiation, and attains union with God through imitating Jesus Christ This state of life, we maintain, needs to rest on a solid foundation; otherwise, it could not endure. Now, this indispensable foundation of the religious life is the Christian life, which precedes the religious life; if that were to be lacking, then the latter would collapse, even though its outward appearance might by chance be maintained for a greater or lesser period.

Christian life consists mainly of two things: *the presence of sanctifying grace in the soul* and *the practice of the teachings of Our Lord Jesus Christ.*

Without sanctifying grace, the soul is dead to God and to itself: with sanctifying grace, it is alive. It would thus be in vain, for any religious who lacked sanctifying grace to imagine that he was fulfilling the obligations of his state of life, even if he tries to be faithful in the practice of his vows and of the Rule. The whole undertaking would have no real basis: and if he did not extricate himself from that unfortunate state as soon as possible, he would run the risk of damnation, the more severe in his case, as he had been favoured with a more holy calling. From this it follows that the religious – as much as, and even more than, the ordinary believer – should shun sin, which banishes grace, and should not simply rely on the holy practices

of his state of life. He should often consider his own frailty, and
the profound malice with which demons attack God's servants,
recalling how it is written, 'Let anyone who thinks that he
stands take heed lest he fall'. Following the Saviour's advice, he
should 'Watch and pray that you may not enter into temptation';
lastly, he should fear and shun those circumstances which he
knows might be dangerous for him, roused to combat by the
reflection that however great the merits acquired by a religious,
only a single mortal sin would be needed to strip him, in an
instant, of all the treasures of grace amassed over many years.

There is thus no distinction at all between the religious
and the ordinary Christian, as to the care needed to preserve
sanctifying grace, unless it be that the religious has yet more
to lose than the ordinary believer, and in misusing a greater
number of graces would find himself placed in a still more
dreadful state by mortal sin.

And since deliberate or habitual venial sin gives rise to a
very great danger of falling into mortal sin, the religious – even
more than the ordinary Christian – will examine his conscience
for venial sin, lest he diminish by his infidelities the abundance
of actual grace, which one needs at every moment, and lose
gradually his sense of the inestimable value of sanctifying
grace.

The brothers will add to their high regard for this greatest
of all good gifts, purchased with the blood of Jesus Christ, a
great esteem for Our Lord's teachings. Since the religious life is
the perfect form of Christianity, and Christianity consists in the
observance of the precepts of Jesus Christ they will endeavour to
keep them with ever-increasing faithfulness. They will take the
greatest care to protect themselves from the illusion into which
many have fallen of convincing themselves that a religious may
be irreproachable, without being perfect as a Christian; they
will frequently examine themselves to discover whether the
efforts they are making to acquire the particular qualities of
a monk are not obscuring their duty to maintain and develop

by grace those qualities which constitute a faithful believer in Jesus Christ To this end, they will make a particular effort to understand the chapter in the holy Rule, *quæ sunt instrumenta bonorum operum*, (on the tools of good works) where our holy Patriarch seems to bring together and weld into a single whole the Ten Commandments, those of the Gospel, and what is taught about perfection.

The theological and the moral virtues should be cultivated by religious, then, with ever-increasing care: their hope of salvation would have been based on these if they had remained in the world, and salvation knows no different conditions in the religious state. The brothers should therefore take these virtues as the basic subject-matter of their daily self-examination, and rely on them in preparing for the sacrament of Penance. The more zeal they show in establishing, maintaining and strengthening the Christian virtues within themselves, the greater will be their desire for religious perfection. What else is that conversion of life and behaviour, which should be the special aim of their profession, if not bringing their whole life into line with the precepts of Jesus Christ, by planting those virtues recommended in the Gospel?

The brothers will therefore consider that a Christian way of life is presupposed by the religious life, and is its indispensable support. An unshakeable foundation for this Christian way of life should first be established on the holy fear of God, which, as the Prophet-king tells us, is 'the beginning of wisdom.' Today's vigourless attitudes seem to want to propose a different foundation for God's service, on sinful man. That is a strange delusion. Yes, it is written that love casts out fear; but who can flatter themselves that they have perfect love? And even if love dispels fear, does that not prove that fear must exist before love? Let the brothers understand the teachings of our holy Patriarch on this subject, and take up this salutary fear for the whole of their lives as the solid basis for the conversion of their life and behaviour, and the best form of protection against backsliding.

They should therefore be happy to meditate on death, the inevitable end of this present life; we do not know the hour it will come, though each moment brings us closer to it; it will establish us for ever, unchangeably, in one eternity or the other. They will be watchful, awaiting the judgement of God, when our faith and our works will be our only defence; a judgement whose sentence will be irrevocable, with no appeal. They will not be afraid to meditate frequently on the eternal pains of hell, on the empty despair of those who will burn there. They will fathom the depths of the justice of God, which did not spare His own Son because He represented sinners; and they will recall the warning of our divine Redeemer, on His way to Calvary: 'If they do this when the wood is green, what will happen when it is dry?'

Following the example of the saints, they will live in continual remembrance of their sins, being all the more careful not to forget them, the more God has been merciful in forgiving them. They must be convinced that the clearest sign of the forgiveness they have received will always be the compunction they should constantly experience; and they should avoid that levity shown nowadays by many people, who seem to think nothing of their sins after absolution; as if it were not written that sin, although forgiven, should continue to inspire genuine fear in the soul of the sinner. We cannot say of such people that love has cast out fear, since we can see that they have no love at all, or very little.

The brothers will find another most powerful reason for fostering the salutary fear of God, when they reflect on the way that they are dependent upon divine grace and the terrible risk they would run by its misuse. Grace is given to everyone, but it does not come to fruition in everyone, because man has the power to put obstacles in its way and block its operations. This divine and merciful grace has come down upon them; it has converted them and put them in the most perfect and surest way to salvation. As sanctifying grace, it could suddenly be extinguished by a single mortal sin and leave the soul to death and damnation. As actual grace, it might become weak, infrequent and barely sufficient as a result of a man's inclination to venial sin and the soul's frequent resistance. When that happens, then the soul, accustomed to more powerful help, surrounded with enemies and snares, will surely fall victim to them, sooner or later, and will then have no reason to complain against God, who owes nothing to the creature whom He has seen scorning the invaluable help that He has continuously bestowed.

The fear of God is thus a well-founded sentiment, and the buttress of the entire edifice of perfection; it is extremely necessary to the soul, even in the most advanced states of spiritual life, since we see it is aroused by God most energetically in the angelic Saint Teresa, when she emerged from the ecstasies which were the reward for her love.

The brothers should use every possible means to avoid becoming insensitive to the promptings of the fear of God, one of the most dangerous symptoms to be seen in a soul. The heart of man is both hard, and frivolous; supernatural fear is the best means to soften, tame and strengthen it. Experience shows that conversions resulting from feeling alone do not persist, unless this blessed fear, in one form or another, comes to shield man against inconstancy, indifference and pride.

Following the example of the Desert Fathers, who withdrew into solitude to meditate on and prepare for the judgement of God, the brothers will often take the teaching of this particular chapter as the subject of their meditations and will soon experience how precious is the fear of God. Then, seeing them sincerely humble at the thought of His fearsome judgement, the Lord will gently transform this first feeling, so that they will pass from fear of His wrath because He is awesome, to fear of offending Him because He is good. Most seriously and firmly resolved to walk in the way appropriate for sinners, they will be called by God's mercy to rise higher to follow the path of trust, a trust that will be all the more sure, in that it has developed in a soul profoundly moved, and firmly established in the only true reality, by the most lawful, formidable fear that can stir men here below.

Humility will henceforth be firmly founded within them, for no other virtue so well prepares the soul for true love of God, and union with Him. To whatever degree of charity they may attain, they will take care to reanimate their courage and constancy by the contemplation of the fearsome judgements of the Lord.

Thus, by constant application of the maxims in this chapter to their spiritual lives, they will become solid Christians: this is the foundation of the religious life, outside of which there is only danger and illusion.

chapter IV

On Faith

THE fear of God, so necessary to every Christian, docility to the teachings of our Saviour, the study of His precepts and the avoidance of what He forbids – all that is based on the virtue of faith, which alone reveals to us Jesus Christ, His rights over us, and what we should fear if we do not listen to His voice.

Faith is the beginning of our salvation: by faith we have been brought into a relationship with God, without it we should remain in darkness; if faith is alive within us, we are bathed in light; if it is weak, everything in our soul is languid. That is why the Apostle tells us that 'without faith it is impossible to please God.'

Now, the ordinary believer cannot remain in relation with God except by means of this virtue, which makes present for him those sublime motives which should order his life. How, then, could any religious persist and advance in the most perfect way, which he must constantly pursue, without a lively faith? The brothers should thus be persuaded of the great need they have of this virtue, and of constant progress in it. To that end, they should first turn to God, asking Him, like the Apostles, to increase this marvellous gift within them; saying to Him with them, *Domine, adauge nobis fidem* (Lord, increase our faith). In their lives they will constantly aspire towards supernatural things, trying to see everything and to judge everything from the standpoint of faith alone, which is that of God Himself; God has deigned to put His own light within our reach, to prevent our reason from going astray and our corrupt nature from falling into error.

Understanding that the state to which they aspire is folly in the eyes of the world, the brothers will very soon come to feel that they can make a success of it only if they are constantly aligning their thoughts, impressions, even their instincts, in the light of the life and the actions of Our Lord, which are in opposition to what is purely natural; in the light of the holy Rule, which involves conditions altogether contrary to those urged by our natural inclinations; and lastly, in the light of the saints, who have trampled nature underfoot, because foolish in the eyes of the world, they were wise with the wisdom of God.

The brothers should use every possible means to bring their thoughts and intentions into line with the thoughts and intentions of Jesus Christ and the Saints. Thus they will establish themselves firmly on the foundation of faith, which will assure the safety of their whole spiritual edifice. They will soon experience that, as long as this foundation remains, their perseverance is certain; but, should it become weakened, they would then become ordinary men, unable to keep their footing in a region to which they had been guided by faith alone, and where only faith can uphold them. The Prophet tells us that 'the righteous shall live by his faith': if this prophecy is true of the ordinary Christian, how much more of the religious! Faith is the natural element of the religious, his food, his joy, and his delight; it is first and principally through faith that God communicates Himself to him and through faith that He makes his life positively heavenly.

In this divine light, those brothers faithful to grace will feel the scales falling from their eyes little by little, and new prospects will be revealed to them. The world and this present life will be transformed before their eyes. They will see clearly that God is everything, and the creature is nothing. The loving kindness of God, the honour and happiness that come with self-denial, renouncing their own selves for His sake, the insignificance of the sacrifices involved in following Him – all that will become clear, and they will be filled with happiness and a holy liberty. All these blessings they will owe to faith, its holy enthusiasm will live in them, ceaselessly renewed by their gratitude to God, who has given them His light, and by continual prayer to Him for the increase in them of this priceless gift.

Henceforward, all their words and actions will be stamped with this element of faith; they will be responsive to everything that promotes it, and they will shrink from that which opposes or hinders it. From this arises a supreme reverence for all that touches God, a tender veneration for holy things, even the least of them. Those objects sanctified by the prayers of the Church, anything which relates, directly or indirectly, to the supernatural, will be especially dear to them. They will be kept safe from a thousand dangers by this blessed *ambiance* which the spirit of faith forms around a faithful soul, and will be able to hear more clearly the voice of God within them. Another result of this state, which should be that in which any Christian finds himself, is a considerable reduction in the devil's power over the soul, which he generally attacks by awakening the spirit of rationalism or of naturalism, something neutralised instantly by the spirit of faith.

The brothers ought to understand that this faith they need so much does not consist only in the intellectual conviction given by study and experience; they will, no doubt, have had to make use of their intelligence, so far as God has thus endowed them, to establish that unshakeable conviction of the fact of divine revelation, and the reality of the mysteries by means of which God condescends to come into relation with man. Yet it is easy to see, in practice, that this kind of faith is not enough to sanctify man. The demons and the damned in hell have this faith, and it neither saves nor converts them. It is the virtue of faith which saves and converts: not the more or less learned deduction of teachers' arguments. The Christian believes because he wants to believe, because he is humble before God, because he knows that God imparts His light to the pure of heart, and that the faith of the mind remains sterile, unless it is, still more, the faith of the heart.

The religious ought to aspire to this virtue, as his primary necessity, since he will need to make more use of it, so to speak, than an ordinary believer. He is called to closer union with God, who dwells in inaccessible light, in the midst of which we must close our mortal eyes in love and trust, to avoid being blinded. It follows from this that the religious should profess unbounded loyalty to Holy Church, whom her divine Spouse has entrusted with the task of leading us to that light. The brothers should not rest content with offering a submission of their mind to the formal decisions of her whom the Apostle calls 'the pillar and bulwark of the truth': they should incline their very hearts to all those devout observances which she encourages; they should look with abhorrence on everything that deviates from this, assured that if they are at one with her in the least details then they are safe. Striving to learn all the ways by which the Spirit of God is at work in her, they will hasten to conform in mind and heart to the least expression of her wishes and thoughts. And since the heart of the truth and the life of Holy Church is the Apostolic See, the brothers will express a devoted love for all the prerogatives of the Roman Pontiff, to his infallibility in teaching and to his divine and immediate authority over the entire Church, which is greater than the authority of any other power on earth, even that of an ecumenical council, because he is the true Vicar of Jesus Christ. They will avoid at all costs the contrary teaching, which is incompatible with true knowledge as well as with the spirit of faith;[9] this being so, if they were unable to rid themselves of the prejudices on this point which they may have developed whilst still in the world, then they should rather withdraw themselves from the Novitiate, than injure themselves and others by remaining in an association

---

[9] These pages were written long before the [First] Vatican Council. Dom Guéranger, however, when he restored the Benedictine Order in France, had demanded as a condition for admission to the Novitiate – as we see – an explicit declaration of faith in the infallibility of the Supreme Pontiff.

whose first rule consists in adherence to the Roman teaching about the divinely established monarchy of the Church.

Finding them all united in the bond of wholehearted submission to the Spouse of Jesus Christ, the divine Saviour will pour down upon them this spirit of faith, which will become a reservoir of all graces, the source of a supernatural illumination, which will guide and strengthen them in all things; and prepare them to gaze eternally and without veil, on that ineffable light whose faintest rays they had prized so highly in this mortal life.

chapter V

On Hope

THE thought of the infinite blessings promised by faith should arouse in us a desire for that supreme Good which faith reveals, and the beauty of virtue should incite our hearts to seek it in every possible way.

Faith is a light destined not only to shine before us; it should also guide our steps and bring us to another virtue which is essential for the Christian, and still more so for the monk: the virtue of hope. Without this virtue, the Christian does not exist, and to be a monk is impossible. But he whose soul abounds in hope is on the way which leads to his final end.

Hope is the firm and supernatural trust that God will graciously help us to arrive at a happy eternity, if we make good use of His grace; and, at the same time, that He will always grant us His grace in proportion to our need of it, provided we ask for it in humility.

The brothers will understand that, since God's loving kindness towards His creatures is infinite, and manifested in works of the most sublime mercy, He demands this confidence in Him by which we render Him justice. The power of this hope is such that the Apostle does not hesitate to say of Christians, 'by this hope we were saved.' Now, as an ordinary believer is supported in God's service by bravely trusting that the Lord will grant him the grace and strength he needs, so also, the religious, for stronger reasons, will persevere on his higher way, more or less easily, according to whether this virtue is more or less dominant within him.

The brothers must therefore apply themselves courageously to the practice of hope: Hope is a virtue because it cannot persist within us unless we succeed in defending it against two enemies which constantly threaten it and with which we must constantly struggle.

The first of these enemies is want of confidence, which would lead us to place too little reliance on the help of grace to achieve all that is demanded of us as Christians and as religious. It is on this side that the devil sometimes attacks the best and most supernatural vocations. In dramatic fashion, often with exaggerations, he vividly depicts those sacrifices we must make, right up to our death, to reach the perfection that God expects from us; he reminds us of our weakness, of our unfaithfulness in the past, of the little energy we have. At the same time, taking great care to hide from our view the all-powerful goodness of God, and His generosity towards the soul who consents to trust in him, he succeeds in shaking the firmest human resolve, and bringing us to within a whisker of being lost. By means of this treacherous scheme he succeeds in depriving an immense number of Christians of salvation, and manages to frustrate the vocations of many souls who are called to the religious life.

So, when the brothers hear the hissing of the ancient serpent, they must be sure to stop their ears, because this mistrust he is trying to arouse in them is a hateful blasphemy against the loving kindness of God. They should consider that, although nothing is truer than the reluctance of nature to espouse what is good, and still more, what is better; though nothing is more real than their weakness and natural faint-heartedness, yet there is something that is still truer, namely the promise God has given us of His grace which is always more powerful than nature. There is always something even more real, namely the constancy with which God makes this grace available to us, and the means by which we may ever increase it, by humbly and persistently imploring it.

Renewed by this thought, suggested by their faith in the word of God, the brothers will bless the Lord, who has taught us that despair is the only sin which cannot be forgiven; revealing to us that hope has the power to move Him, and can open to every soul the path of reconciliation with its Creator. They will therefore never allow themselves to be intimidated in the practice of this virtue, which the Apostle compares to the anchor of salvation, protecting the ship against the raging storms; and they will always hold fast to the saying of our holy Patriarch, that the Novice 'should never lose hope in God's mercy' *(et de Dei misericordia nunquam desperare)*.

Yet there is another danger no less threatening to the virtue of hope, if the brothers did not take care to avoid it. This reef upon which many have been shipwrecked, is presumption. Mistrust wounds God in His goodness, and presumption attacks his honour. It seems to tell Him that man has no need of grace, or that he has such a right to God's help, that he need not worry about it. This attitude constitutes the greatest danger to the brothers' vocation, and even to their salvation.

If they were to lose their sense of being utterly dependent upon God's grace, not only to advance but even to maintain their position, then the brothers would run the risk of letting themselves drift into presumption, to the great detriment of their soul; for they depend on grace not only for what pertains to the lasting state of their souls, but indeed for every action in particular. They will, therefore, often reflect upon the depths of their unworthiness, and on the measureless depths of the goodness of God, who has the right to impart its treasures only to humble souls who unceasingly beseeching Him, and who may refuse them daily to anyone who is so sadly blinded by presumption. Now, anyone who ceases to humble himself, and ask for God's grace with fervour, is close to succumbing to this dangerous vice. Thus the brothers must watch carefully that they be not lulled into any false confidence take possession of them, for sooner or later this would cruelly betray them.

Assured, on the one hand, of the inexhaustible goodness of God who glories in saving and in sanctifying His creature, so as to bring him to glory, and convinced, on the other hand, that humble and confident prayer will win everything without exception from this heavenly munificence, then the smaller they are before God, the more they will experience the blessing of hope. This virtue will keep alive within them a joyful heart, an inner sweetness, a most profound peace, the anticipation of possessing the infinite bliss which awaits them, and finally, the courage they need to overcome themselves in all things; and by this path and the light of faith, they will draw nearer to God, whom they are called to possess by love.

chapter VI

On God's Love

OUR Lord was not satisfied with displaying the light of His eternal truth before our eyes; at the same time He encouraged us to hope for those good things revealed by faith, and deigned to call us to unite ourselves to Him by love. 'The purpose of this instruction,' says the Apostle, 'is love.' And fearing lest we should look on this mutual love between God and man as something audacious, altogether above our nature, the Lord even commanded us to love, on pain of being eternally cast out from His presence. 'You shall love the Lord your God,' he says, 'with all your heart, and with all your soul, and with all your mind, and with all your strength'; and the Lord teaches us that this is the greatest commandment, and first among them all.

Considering the greatnesss and urgency of this instruction, the brothers will henceforward look upon the religious state as that most helpful for fulfilling it and bless God, who has condescended to grant them the gift of a vocation.

The love of God is the whole of the Christian life; the other moral or theological virtues only prepare or help us to love God. St Augustine says, 'Love, and do what you will'; for anyone who truly loves God is protected against sin, since sin is contrary to the love of God. To love God is the easiest and most pleasant of all the commandments, though it is the one that man transgresses most easily and most often. Love of God puts us in possession of God Himself: it is by love that heaven is heaven. It is the prime necessity of our being, since we can be happy only in loving what is good, and that good is God. Loving God is a sacred obligation, since God loves us first, and constantly acts out of love for us, and awaits generously and patiently the response that we owe Him.

The obstacle that God's love encounters within man arises from a variety of causes that arrest the creature in its flight and divert him from his final end, outside of which there is only damnation; for anyone who has not loved God on earth will be brought to the point of hating him eternally in hell. These causes are: *illusions*, which cause us to forget that God invites us to love Him; *the world*, its maxims and the example it gives; *attachment* to material goods, to creatures and to oneself; finally, *lack of support and encouragement*. The brothers will realise, with gratitude, that the religious life removes all these obstacles and makes it easy for anyone who is willing to profit by the means it offers, to fulfil this first and greatest of God's commandments.

The religious life establishes a man in recollection and peace, as on a mountain whose peak almost touches the sky: it provides the soul with that interior and exterior silence, in which the word of God can work, dissipating illusions and protecting the soul against the hidden approach of oblivion. By separating the religious from contact with the world, it keeps him safe from the dangers which that deceitful enemy prescribes in its maxims and example, avoided with difficulty by those who live in its midst. Since any attachment to material goods, to other creatures, and to oneself, is countered by the practice of the holy vows, the soul rediscovers its original freedom and tends with ease towards its divine centre. Supported in every possible way by the Rule and observances, which are a source of countless graces, the soul is strengthened by the example of others and recalled to its true self by exhortations, and if necessary by reprimands and corrections; in order to depart from the way of love it would have to make stubborn and repeated efforts contrary to what is good, something that is fortunately rare.

It follows from this that the religious has greater assurance than anyone else in this world of perseverance in the practice of this commandment; if only on this account, he should consider himself the happiest of men.

The brothers should resolve to take advantage of all these aids for making progress in the love of the Lord their God, so that everything comes down to this one blessed end. It is important that to understand above all that the commandment of this love requires no laborious efforts; as the Lord himself says to his people: 'This commandment which I command you this day is not too hard for you, neither is it far off. It is not in heaven, that you should say, "Who will go up for us to heaven, and bring it to us, that we may hear it and do it?" Neither is it beyond the sea, that you should say, "Who will go over the sea for us, and bring it to us, that we may hear it and do it?" But the word is very near you; it is in your mouth and in your heart, so that you can do it.' We have only to follow the impulse of our heart. To love God then, and the mere thought of His supreme kindness, the mere remembrance of His acts of goodness, will suffice to maintain in us that charity which unites us with Him.

The brothers should be ever intent to profit from everything that increases within themselves this treasure of eternal life and to make, as often as they can, explicit acts which express their love toward God: arising from an impulse of grace, these acts have great power to increase the source from which they come. In all the motives of their actions and thoughts, they should give preference to the of love of God; they will find this a powerful help, and at the same time their thoughts and actions will be raised to greater merit and higher dignity. They should make it their habit to decide in favour of the sacrifices they may have to make, by considering the love they owe to God; for, if this love is real, it should move them to sacrifice and not to taking their ease.

Since God prescribes for man the practice of several distinct moral and theological virtues, they will not dispense themselves from carrying out any of these, on the pretext that the love of God is enough; yet they will try to unite this motive of God with those peculiar to the other virtues, by making them participate in the nature of divine love. Finally, when they happen to commit some fault, they will look on this as being unfaithful to the love they owe to God: this will powerfully serve to hasten the pardon which the Lord will mercifully grant them.

The brothers should be eager to ensure that the motives of their love for God are as perfect as possible. Thus, they will not be content with a purely self-interested love, interested only in their personal beatitude. Without ever ceasing to love God as their final end, with the love of desire which springs from the holy virtue of hope, as its pure and holy source; without halting in its course that grateful love which should fill them with ever-growing awareness of God's blessings towards them; they will reflect that there exists within God an infinite loveliness which rightly arouses our love, quite apart from our own interests; and they will endeavour to rise, as far as their weakness permits, to love God in this way for His own sake, which cancels sin by destroying both the fault and the penalty at the same time, and which can unite, even in this life, the soul to God.

To this end, they should strive to make, according to the inspiration of grace, acts of love and benevolence, of loving kindness and of compassion, by which the soul embraces the interests of God, with an ardour undimmed by self-interest. They should explore the meaning of the Lord's Prayer, the first three petitions of which express this love for anyone able to understand them. In a word, they will act in all things with the conviction that as men, as Christians, and as religious, they have a lofty and universal duty to fulfil in this world, namely the duty of loving God above all, with a constant love, a love which, when all is said, is proportionate to the graces bestowed on them for the purpose of loving Him.

chapter VII

On the Love of Our Lord Jesus Christ

SUCH is the infinite generosity and love of God for us, that we have seen Him come down to the condition of man, to bridge the gap, so to speak, which separated us from Him in order to obtain more effectively the return which is His due. 'For God so loved the world that He gave His only Son.' And the Son of God, already in the Old Testament speaking on the theme of His future coming in the flesh, said, 'My delight was to be with the sons of men.' The brothers should realise, with astonishment and respect, what advances God has deigned to make towards us; and reflecting that He Himself took our own flesh through the divine Incarnation, they will understand how much easier it has become to follow the commandment of loving God; they will frequently thank the Divine Goodness for allowing them to be born after the accomplishment of the mystery of the Word made flesh, which has so greatly opened the path which leads to union with God through love. Jesus Christ is man like us, and anyone who loves Jesus Christ is already in possession of the love of God, because Jesus Christ is God.

And how is it possible for man not to love the incarnate God? The Son of God manifests Himself to us in that delightful state, with so many attractions that, not to love Him, man must either renounce his own nature, or admit that he was quite depraved. There are in fact two reasons which urge us to love those who are like ourselves: their personal charm, and the acts of kindness which they have lavished upon us. Now, can anyone fail to be attracted, when they read and reflect upon the Holy Gospels, by the divine fascination emanating from the words and actions of Our Lord? If we think about Him as a child, what could be more attractive than Him in the manger, or in the arms of His most pure Mother? If we follow Him through His life as a man, then what is more touching than His generosity, His compassion for the tribulations of humanity, His patience, His condescension, and that gentleness which so sweetly tempers the gravity in His person, that it gathers close around Him even little children? What could be more captivating than His teaching, in which the authority of God conceals itself behind the simplest language, in which the most dramatic and sublime truths go straight to the hearts of his listeners, flooding their minds with the most vivid light? What could be more touching, than His partiality for sinners, those unfortunate sick for whom He is the sympathetic physician, lost sheep for whom He has become the tireless shepherd? What could be more moving than the calmness with which He goes forward towards the death that He foreknew, without ever protesting against the ingratitude of His enemies?

For the man with an upright heart who reflects upon that sublime life – and monks should be constantly seeking to understand it more fully – it is impossible not to feel touched, and then completely won over, by the love of Him who led that life on earth. If anyone is moved when he sees one of those traits which reveal a noble sentiment in another person, so much so that his heart beats faster for the sake of that man he will never see, who perhaps has ceased to live on this earth for centuries, then how can we shut out of our hearts love for Jesus, in Whom everything is perfect, everything is whole, everything is inspired by the most generous love for us? Now, in loving Jesus, it is God whom we love. The great commandment to love has come to us, as if to entrap us, and we have been captured: whoever loves Mary's son, loves the Son of God; whoever loves the Son of God loves the Father and the Holy Spirit, for all three are *one*, in a single substance.

Yet if, without turning our gaze away from the ineffable attractions of our heavenly Friend, we come to consider His acts of kindness, how could His love fail to overcome the indifference of our hearts? We were His enemies, and He died for us that death on the Cross. We were lost for all eternity, and He saved us by giving Himself up for us. It was our sins which crucified Him, and He has been glorified in forgiving us. The least reparation offered by Him would have sufficed superabundantly for the offence committed by thousands of worlds against the divine majesty, but to assure our devotion, He was willing to pour out His blood, to the last drop, in the midst of the most horrible pains. His sacrifice, offered for the entire human race, was just as clearly offered for each one of us, as if each of us had been the only one who was guilty and the sole reason for His coming into the world.

Is it not obvious, that he who continually reflects within himself on such reasons for loving Our Lord would be the very last and least of men, undeserving of life if he does not feel invaded by that love? And is it not also true, that he whose heart is not entirely ruined by self-love, or weighed down with the ignoble burden of sensuality, could not recall the man-God's acts of kindness to him, without feeling drawn by love for such a benefactor, a love surpassing that love he feels for his own self?

Then let us say it once more: the great commandment has been fulfilled; the mysteries of the incarnate Word have been the divine bait which lured us. While following the natural bent of our hearts, which inclines us to love others for their attractions and acts of kindness, we have come by way of Jesus Christ, the God–man, to love of the invisible God, who created us to love Him and to serve Him.

The brothers ought easily to understand the ways which the Lord has happily made available to them to fulfil this commandment, fundamental to the Christian life and to the religious life. They will perceive that everything depends on the firmness and the constancy of their love for Our Lord. They will thus have to say, along with the Apostle, 'Who shall separate us from the love of Christ?' And so as to strengthen and increase this love within their souls, they will neglect no possible way of preserving within them the impression of the attractiveness and benefits of the incarnate Son of God. They will make all this the most ordinary subject of their thoughts and affections. To that end, they will work at making progress in their understanding of the Holy Gospel, which will be for them truly good news, since they will learn from it the art of loving God, by loving the divine Redeemer who was so forthcoming towards us.

chapter VIII

On Perfection

IN revealing himself to man through faith, in arousing his hopes of an eternal reunion with the sovereign Good, and in commanding him to love his Creator and his Redeemer, God had in mind an aim relating in the first place to the condition of man in this world. God's aim is that man, in this life, should aspire to perfection.

Perfection is the close and complete correlation of the creature with God, so far as the former's capacities permit. It is the result of the creature's conforming to the holiness of God, by being set free from sin and through genuine practice of the virtues, among which love is the highest, and the one whose influence is shed over all the others.

It follows, then, that there is for the Christian a real duty of desiring perfection, and of striving to practise it, in accordance with the graces he may receive: otherwise, we would have to say that God is not concerned as to whether his creature carries out the project He conceived, or that the creature has every right to deny God the fulfilment of that plan for which He drew him forth from nothingness and redeemed him from hell. Nothing could be more hateful, nor more stupid; and in order that the Christian should entertain no illusions about the commandment concerning perfection, which encompasses all the others, Our Lord said, 'You, therefore, must be perfect, as your heavenly Father is perfect'; and, by this one saying, He showed us the model by which we ought to regulate not only our acts, but also our thoughts and our aspirations.

Fully persuaded that this teaching is true, the brothers should look carefully at their past life, and will realise that they have never committed a single sin without losing sight, at least for the moment, of their duty to be perfect; and that the thought of this duty would, in itself, have been enough to keep them safe from thus falling. They will see clearly that their hope of continuing in the state of sanctifying grace is sure only in the measure that they cherish within themselves the intention of becoming perfect; and that if they were to neglect this intention, or allow it to wilt or fade, then they would set at risk even their eternal salvation. The holiness of their heavenly Father will therefore be the target at which they are aiming. Created and regenerated in the image of God, and destined to be reunited for evermore with Him in that dwelling-place where, as the Apostle says, 'we shall be like Him,' they have no other possible choice here on earth but to make every effort to become like Him, so far as they are able.

Nonetheless, they should not allow themselves to be too cast down if, despite their brave efforts, they can see that they are still far from their divine pattern, as much on account of their past sins, which they have not yet sufficiently expiated, and of the imperfections into which they often fall, as because the target they have set themselves is so infinitely great: yet they will comfort themselves with the reflection that the perfection they have attained is not of this world, and that even the greatest saints have only fully realised it in heaven. What has made them saints is their continuing desire for perfection, a desire and tending never weakened by their faults and imperfections.

The brothers will therefore contemplate this great duty of all Christians with steadfastness, and will pay no heed to the claims of self-love, which would suggest that they give equal weight to God's claims and to those of their own interest (albeit misunderstood). If they reflect on how far the salvation of anyone who gives up the struggle for perfection is put at risk, how far he is straying from the love which is God's due, it will always be easy for them to sustain within themselves, in response to the grace which is never lacking, that firm resolution which will offer both assurance and consolation in their lives.

The devil is constantly attempting to turn aside the desire for perfection in souls, by frightening them with ridiculous imaginings. To hear him, you would think that the path to perfection is nothing but thorns and brambles. The brothers should consider these empty phantoms beneath their notice, and understand better and better that nothing is more right and more sensible for a Christian to do, than to track down sin and its causes within himself, and seek after every virtue, so as to draw near to God, who is infinitely holy, and who has destined us to be united with Him in all eternity. That is what perfection is. It does not consist of this or that extraordinary action, which we may read about in the lives of the saints, and which might seem beyond our powers: it is not on account of those actions that the saints have been saints, but much more because of their persistent desire for perfection, a desire of which those acts were merely a product and expression, varied to some degree in accordance with the kind of graces they possessed.

The brothers ought to feel particularly grateful to God, however, because He has condescended to call them to the Religious life, the school of perfection within holy Church. Religious life is in fact based upon the practice of the evangelical counsels, which aim at destroying those obstacles which so often block the Christian's progress on the path to perfection. Anyone who has seen fit to commit himself to the Lord through holy poverty, chastity and obedience, and who remains faithful to this commitment, is sure to attain to the perfection which assures union with God. That perfection will be his rest, his reward even in this world, and he will discover the truth of Our Lord's word, when he said, 'My yoke is easy and My burden is light.' The obstacles constantly raised up by our own self-love and by our love of objects extraneous to any resolve to become perfect, are cast down by the deliberate and constant practice of this divine teaching; and the love of God, which the holy Apostle calls 'the bond of perfection,' reigns supreme in the soul, and becomes, without difficulty, the soverereign principle of our entire life.

Finally, the brothers will remember that Christians are called to perfection, and the heroic struggles which those who practise this in the midst of the world have to maintain; they will recognise that they have been treated with particularly special favour, in being placed, by their holy calling, on a path in which the light which illuminates every soul will never be lacking for them; in which those graces which support and restore us are poured out upon them hour by hour; so much so, that in order to fail to reach their goal they would not merely have to be incredibly weak, but show a stubborn resistance, from which may God's goodness ever preserve His own.

chapter IX

On the Imitation of Our Lord Jesus Christ

TO ensure our accomplishment of the great and indispensable commandment of love, God deigned, by becoming man, to bring near to us the essential object of our love. By the same mystery of divine Incarnation, He also deemed it appropriate to set well within our reach the model of that perfection that He has made a duty for us. Imitating the perfection of our heavenly Father was very difficult for weak and ignorant creatures; but since the Son of God, who is perfect like the Father, put on the nature of a man and came upon this earth to act, to speak and to will in the ways that a man-God could act, speak and will, henceforth we have had only to imitate Him, to achieve the imitation of God. That is why the Apostle teaches us that 'those whom God foreknew, he also predestined to be conformed to the image of his Son.'

We ought therefore to give thanks without ceasing to the divine mercy, for granting us to be born after the Incarnation of the divine Word; for the light of His example enlightens and guides us, just as His precious Blood has redeemed us. The first man, created in holiness and in justice, no longer exists; sin has made such a ruin of him that the divine features can no longer be recognised: and then Jesus Christ was given to us, not only as a Redeemer, but also as a model. In Him we can recognise what we ought to be in order to resemble God once more. St John, in his Epistle, tells us that what will give us confidence on the day of judgement, is that 'as He is, so are we in this world.' That same Apostle tells us, again, that 'he who says he abides in Him ought to walk in the same way in which He walked.' St Paul explains this in a single phrase, when he says to believers, 'put on the Lord Jesus Christ.'

In gratitude for the ineffable goodness which has deigned to bring us from heaven that model in accordance with which we are to be remoulded, so as to become perfect as our heavenly Father is perfect, nothing will be closer to our hearts than to know that ideal, which is both human and divine, as completely as we possibly can; for this is the ideal which will confront us on the day of judgement. The Saviour puts it like this, speaking to his Father: 'This is eternal life, that they may know Thee the only true God, and Jesus Christ whom Thou hast sent.' From these words all Christians should draw the conclusion that knowing Jesus Christ is the most important thing we can do in this world, since it leads to eternal life.

The brothers should understand, then, that studying Our Lord in the Gospels is the surest way to sustain and encourage within themselves love for this divine Redeemer, just as paying attention to everything He did, everything He said, everything He was, as related in the sacred text, will be the source of that imitation which will bring them to the perfection required by God. To encourage themselves in this search for knowledge, which results in eternal happiness, they will recall what St Luke tells us about the Holy Virgin: that she contemplated the characteristics of Jesus, and kept them in her mind, 'pondering them in her heart.' Through this constant and loving study of Him, Mary succeeded in realising within herself the pattern of her divine Son and rose to perfection. Each follower of Jesus Christ, according to his capacities and calling, should do the same.

The brothers consider it a great honour to have withdrawn from the world with its empty tumult, so that they can study Our Lord in depth, and devote themselves to imitating Him. That will be the subject of their constant reflection, their ceaseless efforts, for if they realise this imitation, they can reckon that everything is won, just as everything would be lost, if they had the misfortune to fail in this. One of the Church Fathers said, without exaggerating, *Christianus alter Christus* (the Christian

– another Christ). What, in fact, is a Christian? He is a member of Jesus Christ. Now, members have the same life, the same inner feelings, as the head.

There is no doubt that this imitation of the man–God, this being incorporated into Jesus Christ, is an arduous undertaking which costs our nature more than one sacrifice; but let us recall that we have no choice. We have to resemble either the earthly or the heavenly man. If we retain the characteristics of the earthly man, we will be set to one side and cast into the fire; if, on the other hand, the Father recognises in us the features of His Son, who is the heavenly man, then He will claim us, too, as His sons, and 'where Jesus is, we shall also be.'

It is true that no one could decide to imitate Jesus, unless he loved Jesus; but have we not seen that loving Him is our foremost duty, the strictest justice, and the dearest consolation in this vale of tears? Determined to be faithful in this love, will easily recognise that nothing is more just than that we should be like Him who took our likeness upon Himself out of love for us. It would be wrong for them to find it hard to reform themselves so as to become more like God Himself, by purifying their lives of all those seeds of evil which would have caused their eternal ruin.

Lastly, they will recall that this reforming of fallen man, on the model of Jesus Christ, is not the work of nature but that of grace, which is always given us and which we can always increase within us by prayer, for God will never refuse any prayer for anything necessary for the progress of our souls. The brothers ought therefore to pray without ceasing that Jesus Christ should take shape within them, that His life be manifested in their lives, and animate their whole being. They will wholeheartedly and faithfully commit themselves to pursuing this as the great aim of their lives, constantly returning to it and taking every opportunity to achieve it. In studying the lives of the most Holy Virgin and of the saints, they will seek out what made these lives holy; and when they see that this is quite simply being conformed to the deeds and the sentiments of Jesus Christ, they will understand, more and more what God expects from them themselves; and in humility and gratitude, they will apply to themselves this saying, which Our Lord addressed to them in the person of St Peter: *sequere me* (follow me).

chapter x

On the Evangelical Counsels

SINCE the imitation of our Lord Jesus Christ is the path that has to be taken by any human creature who wants to achieve salvation and come to glory, the sovereign wisdom of God has determined that this imitation, so exalted in its nature, should be realised in different degrees. Taking human weakness into consideration, and having decided to grant His grace in accordance with His own good pleasure and in perfect harmony, our Lord shared with men His commandments and counsels. The commandments, which everyone has to follow, stand for the essential conditions, without which there is no salvation, the evangelical counsels, are for those who are called to rise still higher in their imitation of our Lord Jesus Christ, who, gave concrete form to the content of these teachings in His own life, with a marvellous fullness and perfection.

Thus, the brothers cannot form too exalted a notion of the evangelical counsels, whether seeing them as having a model in our Lord, or considering them in relation to salvation. From the first point of view, these divine counsels deserve our respect on account of the way they establish a union between our Lord and the person practising them. From the second point of view, it is impossible to form too exalted a conception of their importance, since the practice of the counsels ensures that the commandments are being obeyed, and this is consequently the surest path to salvation. This latter truth is so evident that often, even in the midst of the world, it would be impossible to live the Christian life in practice, without rising in certain instances to the observance of the counsels.

Our Lord gave these divine counsels that they might be followed. Even if He did not make it compulsory for everyone to follow them, He at least desired that a certain number of His faithful should fulfil them. His wisdom and honour are at stake here, as well as the accomplishment of His Gospel, of which not one single *iota* is to remain unfulfilled. To find grace, Earth has constantly to reflect in the sight of God the image of His divine Son, given concrete form in humanity; now, the commandments themselves, even were they to be fulfilled to the letter by all men, would not be enough to reproduce in us the features of the incarnate Son of God. That is why the divine Restorer of the original state of man condescended to use the inducement of a reward, promising a hundredfold to those who observe the counsels, so as to bring with Him, as many as possible of those He has redeemed.

The brothers should offer sincere assent to the merciful intentions of their Redeemer, and give humble thanks to Him, for in calling them to the holy religious life, which is the school of the evangelical counsels, He has set them on a privileged path which fully obtains the glory of God, by the most complete imitation of His Son. They will constantly implore the grace to avoid falling from this higher degree, where the divine grace has set them through no merit of their own, and they will be humbled at the thought that it is no part of God's plan to call all men to the same favour.

They will remember the calling of the Apostles, who were the first to be chosen to leave everything and devote themselves not just to the Saviour's commands but also to His counsels. Their reward was first of all to live in close familiarity with their divine Master, to share His secrets, to co-operate in His mission: at the end of time they will be seen sitting on thrones to judge the twelve tribes of Israel. A similar destiny is reserved for those who imitate them: an intimate relationship with Jesus, who will have no secrets from them, and the highest distinctions in the eternal kingdom.

Turning next to look at their own weakness, which they know from experience, the brothers should acknowledge how much they owe to divine mercy, which – desiring to ensure their salvation – has set them firmly in the path most certain to take them to this goal, which is the one thing necessary. The practice of the counsels, which is so greatly facilitated in the religious life, will certainly win them the most precious merits, and will also guarantee obedience to the commandments. Thus they will gain both salvation and perfection together. For that is the effect of a religious vocation: when man takes it up with a good will, it brings him to the sovereign Good much more easily than in the midst of the world, where everything constitutes an obstacle, whereas in the religious life everything helps.

They will then see quite clearly that a religious vocation is a path open, in God's mercy, to a great many souls, even though few follow it. God calls souls to the religious life, in fact, sometimes by attraction, and sometimes by external circumstances. It is He who inspires the attraction; it is His grace which gives rise to the circumstances. He calls both the righteous and sinners: the righteous, that they may satisfy the hunger and slake the thirst they have for justice; the sinners, that they may become righteous and holy. Such wonders of grace as these result from the practice of the evangelical counsels, which elevates the whole of one's life and transform it in Jesus Christ.

Thus, the brothers will become aware of the essence of the religious vocation, which is so different from the vocation to priesthood. The latter depends on God alone, who is the only one who can choose His ministers – that is, those whom He wishes to set in place as mediators between God and men. The former, on the contrary, depends both on divine grace and on ourselves. Faith enlightens us concerning how good the life of perfection is, and grace urges us to take it up and gives us the strength to do so. Man either follows this attraction, or he does not; and so it is that in the Gospel we see our Lord inviting men to follow the way of the counsels, but where the priesthood is concerned, He himself makes the choice. It follows that no authority in the world, whether natural or even ecclesiastical, has the right to hold anyone back if he wants to take up the way of the counsels; for no one has the right to prevent a righteous man from coming closer to God, or the sinner from taking up the means which will ensure the conversion of his life and his progresses towards what is good.

§ I

on holy poverty

THE evangelical counsels may be summed up in three principle ones, the first of which is *poverty*, that is, a complete and unconditional renunciation of possessing any earthly things, whether valuable or otherwise. Holy poverty is the first degree in the perfect imitation of our Saviour. He was born in a borrowed stable, and worked by the sweat of His brow to get the food He ate; He lived on alms while He was preaching; He was nailed naked to the Cross; and His body was laid to rest in a borrowed tomb. It was impossible to show us more clearly that absolute poverty is a path of merit and restoration. This path, in fact, extinguishes the longing for earthly goods within man, which St John calls 'the lust of the eyes,' and which is one of the things that most offends God and most contributes to the ruin of souls. Holy poverty is the beginning of the perfect life; that is why our Lord says, 'If you would be perfect, go, sell what you possess and give to the poor, and you will have treasure in heaven.' There can be no life completely in conformity with Jesus Christ's, without a real despoilment of earthly goods, and holy poverty is the first step we have to take to enter into that blessed life.

Practice has constantly shown that this virtue is the foundation of the whole structure of religious life. Just as we may hope for anything from a religious family within which poverty is practised and held in honour, so equally we must expect that wherever this rule is broken and disregarded, the other foundations of religious life are shaken, and will soon no longer be able to hold. The violation of religious poverty does in fact involve the breaking of an oath, since this poverty is the subject of a vow. Besides that, it is really theft, since anyone who indulges in it has no rights over whatever he is using. No doubt there can be more or less serious instances in practice, according to the value of the thing, but breaking the oath and the act of theft are none the less real.

All religious therefore need to love holy poverty with a genuine love, if they really desire to persevere in practising this holy virtue. And how should they not love it, when they recall the marvellous zeal with which the Saviour Himself practised it, how strictly He enforced it upon the Apostles, and how keen the primitive Church in Jerusalem was to practise it, all aflame with the fire of the Holy Spirit?

Full of respect for this fundamental virtue, and ardently desiring the treasure in heaven promised by our Lord, the brothers will look forward to the day when they will be able to practise this first evangelical counsel in fact. They will acquire a full idea of the nature and practice of this noble holy poverty. Thus, they will understand that those who have made this vow should not allow themselves any regret for what they have left behind, nor any desire or inclination to possess anything at all. To be attached to any objects given them to use – a book, for example, a piece of furniture, or a cell, etc. – would be to fail in practising the poverty they have promised. Any privation one may feel, as long as it is not injurious to health, should cheerfully be endured by the religious, because it is then that he is really living the religious life. For nothing is more contrary to the spirit of monasticism than that foresight with which one might arrange things so that nothing be lacking to him, and to accumulate various objects which are convenient rather than necessary. It is wrong to appropriate for one's own private use things that are not intended for that. Finally, the conscientious duty of any religious is to handle carefully those things that are regularly made available for his use, considering them as objects lent to him, so that he ought in all honesty, and out of consideration for others, to take good care of them.

The brothers, being instructed as to the extent and practice of holy poverty, should prepare themselves for this with holy zeal, and will be happy to renounce in advance any desire for the goods of this world, so that they may possess God. Far from being worried about any possible events of the present time, when the plots of the enemies of our faith are directed mainly against the revival of the religious state, they will feel themselves greatly honoured, when they think that the Lord might count on them, just as He counted on the Apostles, whom He sent out into the world like lambs among wolves, after He had summoned them to leave their boats and their nets.

To show just how simple is their aspiration to be the poor of Jesus Christ, they will begin as soon as possible to omit from their conversation all those words which express the notion of property. They will then begin to make as little use as possible of those articles which belong to them, accustoming themselves to being satisified with what is strictly necessary. If they do happen to lose, destroy, or damage anything at all belonging to the community, they will confess this fault at Chapter and will do penance for it, just like the professed monks. When they feel the effects of the deprivations which religious poverty imposes on us concerning food, furnishings, and so on, they will rejoice in this, thinking that this is what they have sought, and they will gladly become hardened to those sacrifices brought upon them by renouncing comfort and property.

In this way, the brothers will prepare to take their vow of holy poverty, and ripen in the spirit of their vocation. Their best way of maintaining this supernatural attitude will be to meditate upon the vanity of natural goods, from which man is forever separated by death; and to contemplate the life of our Lord, Who (as the Apostle says) being rich, became poor for our sake; and lastly, to recall how many kings and princes, how many queens and princesses, have given up their crowns, their enormous wealth, everything that could indulge the senses or flatter vanity, in order at the end to become poor, and to detach themselves from all that passes away, happy and proud to be like our Saviour, and by this means to win for themselves true riches, a lasting honour, and an eternal treasure.

§ II

on holy chastity

THE second evangelical counsel is that of holy chastity, to which our Lord directs our attention when He praises those who have renounced the pleasures of the senses 'for the sake of the kingdom of heaven.' Similarly, St Paul shows us its importance, when he proposes complete continence as being what is "better" for a man (cf. I Cor. 7:38), because it sanctifies him in body and soul. Yet since chastity is a virtue enjoined upon every man, even outside the holy state of religion – although it achieves its perfection only in that state – it is expedient to explain the whole Christian teaching on that subject here, so that the brothers may grasp in its entirety a subject as important as this.

The aim of the holy virtue of chastity is to order people's sensual desires and to subordinate them to the law of the Spirit. This preserves the dignity of man, and causes his soul always to reflect the image of God, who is spirit. The vice opposed to chastity debases man and reverses the economy of his creation, turning it upside-down so that the coarser element predominates, and the soul is stifled beneath the senses. Nothing could be more completely opposed to what the Creator had in mind. He therefore decided to unite the duty of chastity with the exercise of those rights He assigned to the state of marriage. Thus, it is in obedience to a fundamental principle of his existence that man should constantly strive to free himself from the yoke of his sensual nature. Not only is every exterior action contrary to holy chastity forbidden him; but beyond this, it is enjoined on him to keep safe his heart and his spirit from every wilful desire, or indulgence, with regard to what is forbidden by this virtue. The delicacy of holy chastity is such that no infringement of the obligations it lays upon us can be considered of minor importance where its substance is concerned; only the lack of complete intention, and imperfect consent of the will, can make this a venial sin, rather than the mortal sin it might have been.

It follows that man should devote the whole of his efforts to persevere in the holy virtue of chastity, since it is indispensable to him. Yet two obstacles to this make themselves felt, and enable this virtue to exist in us, only at the cost of a struggle. In the first place, one of the consequences of the original Fall was to lay upon us the burden of concupiscence, which upsets the balance between flesh and spirit, and helps the former gain the upper hand, weak as it is. In the second place, the devil is particularly horrified by the holy virtue of chastity. This is because it humiliates him by showing how man ascends by the Spirit, despite his weakness; and that is why this fallen angel likes to attack us from what he can see is our weakest point.

Man should not reckon his condition as being too hard, however, when he sees how he has to go through real battles for the preservation of such a noble and courageous virtue. God does not lay upon his creature any burden that he cannot bear. However great the weakness of our fallen nature may be, the grace of Jesus Christ is made available to us in overflowing abundance, to make good the balance of forces in the combat. We shall not be tested beyond our strength to endure: God's justice, and goodness guarantee this. Those temptations to which we may be subjected, far from discouraging us or filling us with fear, should inspire us all the more to seek after a virtue against which Satan shows such unbridled rage.

It is the duty of every man to keep himself continent according to his state of life, and to live with respect for a virtue so beautiful and so necessary that an offence against it may plunge man into the most abject degradation, ruin his bodily capacities, darken his reason, and bring him to trample upon his most sacred obligations. But our Lord, Who came to raise up human nature in every respect, has graciously inspired in us a higher way of life, where holy chastity not only serves to sustain the dignity of man and save him from all disorders, but exalts him above his own condition and unites him with God. Happy is he who can understand and savour this, and who has been able to unite with the renunciation of all earthly goods, the absolute renunciation of those sensual pleasures which are allowed and sanctioned by a noble sacrament – although in a lower state – on account of the end associated with them. Happy is he who, through the inspiration of divine grace, has chosen in this life that state which is destined to be that of all the chosen ones in our homeland, where our Saviour tells us we shall be like angels.

The purpose of perfect continence, embraced by man with a view to living in conformity with the second of our Saviour's counsels, is to bring into being within him a new degree of resemblance to his divine model. It involves a sacrifice, and God accepts the homage of that sacrifice with particular pleasure. It does away with that division which, according to St Paul, is the essence of the relative imperfection of even the holiest marriage. It brings about the establishment of an eternal relationship with God, which imprints upon the entire person a sign of glory, a sign which will never fade, a sign which merits for him from God a love not granted to others. It reserves for God no longer just inanimate things, as religious poverty does, but the human creature itself, who is henceforth pledged to God as a wife is to her husband. This is a state of liberty with respect to the senses, which are purified and sanctified, an earthly perfume which effortlessly mingles with that of heaven, something which even pagans honoured.

Accepting such an exalted conception of religious chastity, the brothers will not fail to reflect that, if this virtue vowed by the religious is really so valuable, then any transgression against must constitute a very considerable offence against God. The merit accompanying this virtue, even in its smallest details, is enormous; a transformation of the entire person has been brought about; it is now united with God, by the most sacred covenant and the person's first duty is that of faithfulness. Hence not only would the breaking off of this bond be a dreadful sacrilegious act, but also any sin, whether greater or lesser, which in a man not committed to God would render him culpable, in the case of a religious connotes, over and beyond that, a form of sacrilege, corresponding in degree to the fault committed – just as all offences against conjugal fidelity are tainted with the evil of adultery.

The brothers will therefore take good care to temper, with holy fear, the enthusiasm they should rightly feel about the sublime commitment which brings them a share in the life of the angels. Humbly aspiring to establish the relationship which will bind them to God forever, they will be eager to inquire about the means whereby they will be able to maintain it with honour and faithfulness.

The first of those means consists of recognising, all life long and on every possible occasion, that fallen man cannot by his own strength alone acquire or preserve the heavenly gift of chastity; and that only God can grant this to us and keep it safe in us. We therefore need to call ceaselessly on divine help to assist us, confidently imploring the Lord to continue graciously to lend us His aid, and pleading with renewed insistence whenever the wind of temptation blows. Turning to

Mary for the gift of chastity is all-powerful, for she has received the special prerogative of helping the faithful to preserve that virtue of which she is, before all other creatures, the fullest and most magnificent expression, and is called by the Church the *Virgin of virgins*. A devotion to the holy Angels, to St Joseph, to our holy Patriarch, and to those saints, both men and women, who kept pure the lily of virginity, is likewise a great help in ensuring that the gift of chastity is preserved.

The second means is frequent reception of the holy Eucharist. Since it is the most pure Body of the Son of God incarnate, it possesses the particular virtue of calming within us the rebellion of the flesh. As this majestic sacrament transforms man into Jesus Christ, it weakens concupiscence without delay, spiritualises the inclinations of our heart, illuminates our intelligence, and fills our soul with the awareness of God's holiness and the desire to take this as our standard. The devil is forced to withdraw before his adversary, and – even if he does not at first yield completely – he knows that his rule is under threat, and soon departs from every soul which frequently and worthily turns to such a powerful remedy.

The third means is to preserve within us and increasingly develop, that spirit of faith which continually keeps alive in our thoughts the saving truths revealed by God. Anyone who is ever preoccupied with the loving-kindness God manifested to man in the mysteries of the Incarnation and Redemption; who sets a proper value on the sanctifying grace which assures the eternal possession of God; who trembles at the thought of judgement and hell – that man has nothing to fear. Set firm on the rock of faith, he will not be overthrown by temptation; most often, indeed, it will pass over him without having shaken him.

The fourth means lies in respecting and practising humility. God has established a mysterious connection between this virtue and chastity, just as Satan has made a similar one between pride and impurity. This was noted at an early stage by masters of the spiritual life, and constant experience has proved this true. Let the brothers be humble, then, and it will be easy for them to remain chaste. When labouring under temptation let them be brave in accepting humiliations, seeking them and taking them upon themselves; they will soon feel that Satan has lost all his power over them, and calm will follow the storm.

The fifth means consists of a genuine delicacy of conscience, which takes fright at anything which might threaten holy chastity, whether through the senses or through the imagination. This delicacy, based on a spirit of faithfulness, and not of scrupulousness or narrow–mindedness, and notes the least movements of the enemy, and never feels sure about his intentions, which are always as deceitful as they are hostile. It knows where one's weak areas are, and sets a strong guard upon them. If there has been any warning, any injury – however light – that is enough to ensure constant vigilance in this vulnerable area. Lastly, such sensitivity fears all the illusions of a false conscience, which have been the shipwreck of so many souls.

The sixth means of maintaining chastity lies in continual mastery over one's powers of imagination, by courageously curbing their wanderings. Reserve, and modesty in the way we look at things and people, are absolutely necessary for anyone who wishes to keep themselves chaste, and at the same time they are part of monastic decorum. With respect to all the other senses, firmness of conduct should be extended just as far as experience has shown us that there are any dangers. As for our thoughts and imagination, one has to know how to cut off without delay, not only what might be wrong, but also anything that might be risky, and to be constantly on one's guard against *rêveries* and idle thoughts.

The seventh means consists in the mortification of the body. Hardships voluntarily imposed on the flesh lighten its weight, and check its insolence. By habitually chastening the body, one more easily finds the strength to fight against it. Let the brothers learn from the example of our holy Patriarch who won the struggle for chastity through suffering; let them be constant in practising penance, and they in turn will win a sure and lasting victory over concupiscence.

The eighth means lies in respecting and loving holy chastity. Let not the brothers think of it, then, as a yoke laid upon them, but as a liberation. No doubt, there are souls whom God leads by way of long and great temptations. In doing so, He has in mind His own glory and the triumph of His grace: He uses this kind of testing as a way of keeping these souls safe from perils that would be far more dangerous for them; He keeps them in a state of humility, and opens up for them an enormous source of merits. Yet that is not the way God works with regard to the majority of souls. On the contrary, it has been found that chastity, if loved and kept resolutely guarded, soon becomes easy to practise: senses that have been curbed can be ruled with no great effort, an imagination that is under the sway of the teachings of faith no longer wanders, and a purified heart seeks after God in all simplicity and finds Him. Being morosely preoccupied with chastity is more a danger than a help; let the brothers show themselves simple and straightforward in this and other points, and they will find rest and joy for their souls.

§ III

on holy obedience

THE third and most excellent of the evangelical counsels is holy obedience. This consists in giving up our own will to do that of a superior to whom one freely submits, for the purpose of pleasing God. Religious obedience is thus totally different from that which we owe our parents, imposed by nature, and still more from that of the soldier, which may be merely external, and may yet suffice. Religious obedience should be interior and directly willed, as it derives from the free decision that the religious has made to be pleasing to God; and this obedience unites us intimately with God. Through religious poverty, man parts himself from something that is not himself, in order to walk towards God with an untrammelled step; through religious chastity, he curtails his rights over his own person to draw closer to God; but through religious obedience, he renounces his whole self, by giving up his will, which was limited, it is true, by poverty and chastity, yet which had remained free in all other things. This renunciation is made by putting oneself into God's hands; the religious then becomes the property of God, not only as creature, but as something freely offered and dedicated. Henceforward, there is a contract between God and the soul of the religious, the latter sets the will of God in place of his own, and since God does not manifest His commands in a visible way, but, on the contrary, desires to nourish love within the soul by faith, it seeks and finds God's will in the will of that other creature, to whom it has subordinated itself. It is then that our inmost soul is able to be united to God, and firmly set upon the path of perfect charity, since there can be no closer relation between two free and intelligent beings than that which arises when their two wills are united in a single will. Happy, then, is that soul whom divine grace has helped to understand the inexpressible advantages of renunciation.

Our Lord, in his sacred humanity, gave concrete reality to this perfect obedience, which is the essence of His mortal life, just as it is the essence of the religious, in whom it is the will of Jesus Christ that He should be imitated. If the Son of God has come down to us, then He has 'come,' as He says, 'to do the will of my Father.' Elsewhere He tells us that 'to do the will of Him who sent me' is his 'food'; and to fulfil that will, He 'became obedient unto death, even death on a cross.'

Nothing is more glorious, then, than to follow the example of the Son of God Himself; nothing more conducive to the health of the soul. Sin is our greatest enemy, since it can deprive us of God. Now, sin is the product of self-will. If this will can be fettered, then, so that it is no longer able to move except towards what is good, is it not obvious that sin is cast forth from our lives, wherever this blessed obedience extends? It utterly destroys in our own will whatever is human and dangerous, so as to unite our will to God's, which is always holy and always works in our true interests. Then it is that we fulfil what the Lord has told us to do, when He urges us to 'hate' our 'life in this world' – that is to say, our self-will – and to give it up, if we want to serve Him securely and to cleave to Him closely.

Convinced of this teaching, the brothers should love this virtue of obedience, which brings so many benefits with it. They will love it as their glory, and love it as the basis of their security. Yet they must understand, that in order to practice it perseveringly, they have need, above all, of the spirit of faith. Faith alone can disclose to them the presence of God Himself in the person and orders of their superior. They should therefore live by faith, and rise above that which is flesh and blood: they will then obey with joy and constancy, and their obedience will be acceptable to God.

Thus, they will take good care to become accustomed, right from the start, never to discuss the matter of obedience, but simply to accomplish it, as if they were hearing the direct voice of God, filled with gratitude at His taking such pains to guide them. If what they are ordered to do seems inappropriate to them, they will take steps to dominate their reason and accomplish what is commanded, for the simple reason that the order comes from God. They will take care not to criticise the instructions given them, even interiorly, much less exteriorly; for that would indicate that the spirit of faith was no longer within them, that they had once more become carnal men.

Their obedience will be prompt, courageous and un-hesitating. They will not see the difficulties, and will overcome any repugnances. Nothing more rejoices God's heart than the sight of this abandonment, which demonstrates the loving trust placed in Him by His creature. Thus we ought not to be surprised at the miracles which religious obedience has so often brought about: since it has the effect of uniting in a single action the will of the Creator and that of the creature, what is surprising about God's action, when nothing is hindering Him?

Having constantly before them this great commandment of renunciation which is mentioned in the holy Gospel as the necessary path towards perfection, the brothers will be ready for anything, waiting only for a sign, in order at any given instant to do the opposite of what they were doing a moment before; and carrying out this task or that with the same goodwill, being assured that it does not matter what particular task we do, but solely whatever is God's good pleasure. He reveals to them what pleases Him, and will keep account for eternity of the least signs of self-abnegation offered Him in this world.

Above all, they ought to fear influencing the commands they are given, by showing reluctance. If their Superior, having found them ungenerous in their response, should think it necessary to treat them more carefully than other people when it came to obedience, then they will regard such special consideration as the greatest misfortune that could happen to them; they should humble themselves before God, for having earned this sad privilege and allow themselves no rest until they have won back their right to be subjected to trials, like their brethren, in that virtue which, more than any other, constitutes the essence of any religious.

Let the brothers take the greatest possible care not to be lazy about obedience; those who are narrow-hearted fall into this laziness. It consists of resting content in the enjoyment of one's own will, finding a kind of well-being in the thought that we are doing what we want, and that no order can interfere with our independence. Let them remember what it says in the book of The Imitation of Christ: *Qui se subtrahit ab obedientia, ipse se subtrahit a gratia.* With the exercising of obedience, grace extends its rule within the soul, while merit increases and multiplies;

in the absence of any commands, the soul might easily lose what it has already gained, if it did not take care to keep in good working order this precious means which, day and night, makes it open to grace. Let the brothers frequently examine themselves in the point, then, and let their desire to remain ever in union with God always live within them, to uphold the spirit of a virtue which is the vital principle of religious life.

Let them also beware of one danger to which their obedience might be open, if they were not keeping constant watch over their most intimate inclinations: this danger consists in obeying, not for the love of God, but from human affection for the person who gives the orders. It is true that God often makes obedience easier for religious through the feeling of affection for their superiors which he inspires in them; but whilst still preserving this praiseworthy sentiment, they should strive to elevate and purify it, so that the dominant motive for acting remains a supernatural one and leads them to attain to that merit which God has in mind for them. They will bravely imagine what it might be like, were they under obedience to a Superior for whom they have no sympathy, and they will resolve to act with no less a fidelity in fulfilling their obedience to him. By this means they will acquire that indifference – an indifference both holy and necessary for any religious – through which they will always be ready to have what they wish either granted, or refused, since they will have only one end in view: knowing God's holy will through what is commanded them, and fulfilling it with good grace and determination.

Love for the virtue of obedience will not only make them responsive to the will of their Superior under whose authority God has set them, but will also put them at the service of those who are appointed to guide them, or are responsible for the various departments both of the Novitiate and of the monastery. More than that, they will be zealous in their obedience to our holy Patriarch's directions in the holy Rule, where he formally enjoins monks to be 'obedient to each other,' that self-will might be destroyed utterly, and the spirit of obedience flourish within his children, that spirit of obedience which should set right within them all the damage that their own will has done them.

Filled with respect for this fundamental spirit of the religious life, they will fervently ask the Lord to keep them safe, throughout their lives, from that unfortunate tendency which has hindered the growth of more than one soul in religious life, which consists in discussing just how far one's conscience is involved in resisting the commandment to obey, so as to give way only from fear of committing a formal sin. Those souls, unless they are converted, will never attain the perfection they have vowed to pursue. To please God, obedience, must be the fruit of a soul free from egotism, not the result of a calculation which drags it down into the realms of speculation. Reducing life to a matter of avoiding formal sin, instead of trying to do good for its own sake – is that not making oneself a shameful mercenary, when one could be a child? Does it not rob God of the glory He expects in return for the sublime vocation to which He calls the religious soul? Is it not, in the end, narrowing one's heart, when it ought on the contrary to be enlarged with the feeling of love, whose most noble and most complete expression is perfect obedience?

Let us add, in conclusion, that the vows of poverty and of chastity, which the religious has to practise right up to death, are placed in the keeping of obedience. Anyone who is not obedient from the heart would soon transgress in the matter of poverty, whose holy sacrifices are so often a burden to our will; and how could he be sure of keeping holy chastity for long, unless he were responsive, above all, to the counsels and instructions of obedience, whose aim is to protect him against his own weakness?

From all this, the brothers will conclude that obedience is the most precious treasure of any religious; that he can never love it with too great an ardour, nor ever too vigorously defend it; for it is through obedience that he truly enters into possession of the freedom of the children of God, which is offered to him even in this world, and will earn for him an infinite glory in the next.